THE GAMBLING TIMES GUIDE TO
FOOTBALL HANDICAPPING

By
Bob McCune

D1264870

A GAMBLING TIMES BOOK

DISTRIBUTED BY
LYLE STUART
Secaucus, N.J.

McCUNE, BOB
THE GAMBLING TIMES GUIDE
TO FOOTBALL HANDICAPPING

ISBN: 0-89746-022-7

Distributed by Lyle Stuart, Inc.

Manufactured in the United States of America
Printed and Bound by Kingsport Press
First Printing—March 1984

Editor: *Kelley D. Ritchey*
Cover by Jerome D. Holder

All material presented in this book is offered as information to the reader. No inducement to gamble is intended or implied.

Other *Gambling Times* Books
Available—Current Releases
(See page 143 for details)

Poker Books

According to Doyle
by Doyle Brunson
Caro On Gambling by Mike Caro
Caro's Book of Tells by Mike Caro
The GT Official Rules of Poker
by Mike Caro
Poker For Women by Mike Caro
Poker Without Cards by Mike Caro
Wins, Places and Pros
by Tex Sheahan

Blackjack Books

The Beginner's Guide to Winning
Blackjack by Stanley Roberts
The GT Guide to Blackjack
by Stanley Roberts and others
Million Dollar Blackjack
by Ken Uston

Casino Games

The GT Guide to Casino Games
by Len Miller
The GT Guide to Craps
by N.B. Winkless, Jr.

General Interest Books

According to GT: The Rules of
Gambling Games
by Stanley Roberts

The GT Guide to Gaming Around
the World
The GT Guide to Systems That
Win, Volumes I and II
The GT Guide to Winning
Systems, Volumes I and II
GT Presents Winning Systems and
Methods, Volumes I and II
The Mathematics of Gambling
by Dr. Edward O. Thorp
Odds: Quick and Simple
by Mike Caro
P$yching Out Vegas
by Marvin Karlins, Ph.D.
Winning By Computer
by Dr. Donald Sullivan

Sports Betting Books

The GT Guide to Basketball
Handicapping by Barbara Nathan
The GT Guide to Greyhound
Racing by William E. McBride
The GT Guide to Harness Racing
by Igor Kusyshyn, Ph.D.,
Al Stanley and Sam Dragich
The GT Guide to Jai Alai
by William R. Keevers
The GT Guide to Thoroughbred
Racing by R.G. Denis

The following *Gambling Times* books are scheduled for release in September 1984:

Poker Books

Caro's Poker Encyclopedia
by Mike Caro

**Free Money: How to Win in the
Cardrooms of California**
by Michael Wiesenberg

The Railbird by Rex Jones

Tales Out of Tulsa
by Bobby Baldwin

**World Class Poker, Play by
Play** by Mike Caro

General Interest Books

Caro On Computer Gambling
by Mike Caro

The GT Quiz Book
by Mike Caro

How the Superstars Gamble
by Ron Delpit

**How to Win at Gaming
Tournaments** by Haven Earle Haley

**You're Comped: How to Be a
Casino Guest** by Len Miller

Sports Betting Books

**Fast Track to
Harness Racing Profits**
by Mark Cramer

**Fast Track to
Thoroughbred Profits**
by Mark Cramer

TABLE OF CONTENTS

Acknowledgements

It is my pleasure and responsibility to acknowledge the following aid and assistance in formulating the ideas, concepts and work that comprise this book.

First and foremost, I wish to thank my wife, Maisie, for the many hours she spent deciphering and editing my original longhand drafts, which she inputted into the computer. I also wish to thank Joan Pettit, my secretary and computer operator, for her assistance in resolving the final draft after many editing sessions.

There are many others to whom I owe a grateful thank you for their help and contributions. Paul Shullo, one of my most loyal and capable employees, for his suggestions and assistance in organizing and editing of the manuscript. Another who has directly contributed to many of the ideas that went into the book is Jim Pettit. Jim has sixteen years of experience as a professional handicapper. He is also a first-rate sports analyst whose abilities have enlightened me to many truths in the sports betting industry.

Thanks also to Sonny Reizner, manager of the "Hole in the Wall" Sports Book at the Castaways, for what he has taught me in our many rap sessions and interviews over the last few years. Other individuals who have served as my mentors and indirect contributors are Jack Painter, John Hodges, Martin Mendelsohn, Dana Allen, Rick Hall, Barbara Nathan, Jim Longnecker and many others whose books, newsletters, articles and conversations have helped me accumulate the overall knowledge and awareness of the subject which I presently enjoy.

Finally, I wish to thank the President of Gambling Times Incorporated, Stan Sludikoff, for asking me and contracting with me to write this book; otherwise its publication at this time would have been neither practical nor possible.

Preface

Given the nature of the books available on football handicapping and sports wagering, this book is an innovative and much-needed addition. Other books have been written from the perspective of how to win, how to use a system or what the past records and statistics indicate. However, *The Gambling Times Guide to Football Handicapping* is written from the perspective of how "the system" works and what you need to do to assure that you are the one with the edge. In football handicapping and wagering, there are elements working against the player. Bob makes sure players are aware of these factors, so they can better perform in the sports betting marketplace.

One of the reasons Bob has been able to carry off this approach to writing a book on football handicapping is that he does not look upon himself as just a professional handicapper. That is, he doesn't do all the detail work himself. In the operation of his sports service, Bob employs the services of those who make their livelihood picking winners from the schedule, while he tries to concentrate on the position of "running a business." This gives him a much broader perspective of the handicapping and wagering scene than many others buried within the selection process. In using the handicapping talents of others and translating their selections into a winning program for clients, Bob has had to become aware of all the facets of handicapping, wagering, money management, winning and interacting with a public that only understands "winners" and not "winning."

Bob McCune has had a long association with sports, dating back to his youth when he excelled in hockey and was drafted by the New York Rangers. World War II intervened and after a Navy stint Bob ended up in the San Francisco area where he opened a gym and later matriculated at Stanford University. In 1949, he won the title of Professional Mr. America and parlayed the title and his athletic abilities into a nine-year career as a professional wrestler. He toured the world and among his 1200-plus matches, nine were for the world championship against Lou Thez. Bob became a division manager and the all-time number one salesman for Great Books after he retired from wrestling.

Bob's next entry into sports was a series of mini-tours of professional golf in Florida and Georgia in the early 1970s. In 1975 he moved to Las Vegas and became involved in sports betting because of his love of sports and the excitement associated with a little action on his favorite teams. He found that sports wagering also satisfied his needs to be analytical, pragmatic and a winner.

McCune became involved in the sports advisory business in 1980 and opened The Vegas Sports Information Center early in 1981, which he has since dissolved in favor of playing the games himself and handling only a few select private clients. Because he perceives himself as a winner, Bob feels he can make anyone else a winner, provided they follow his advice. Since entering the sports service arena, Bob has become a frequent contributor to sports wagering publications. He has edited a newsletter and fact sheet called *The Profit Line* and presently edits a publication called *The Sports Investor*. He has also written for many other publications, including *The Experts, Gambling Times, Sports Form* and *Las Vegan*.

The Gambling Times Guide to Football Handicapping should be in every sports enthusiast's library and be one of the elements that makes for a better experience for the sports bettor and handicapper. With your acquisition of this book, you have made a positive step towards improving your "winning edge."

John Hodges
Associate Director
American Association of
Documented Sports Services

★ ★ ★

Publisher's Note: Since Bob McCune completed this book in the fall of 1983, he has dissolved The Vegas Sports Information Center and is now involved in private sports handicapping and personal betting. He handles a few select clients and would be more than happy to assist anyone in need of his advice and talents. Bob can be reached at his Las Vegas office by calling (702) 870-6665, or by writing to Bob McCune Sports Investments, 4535 W. Sahara, Suite 105, Las Vegas, NV 89102. Bob can also be reached through *Gambling Times.*

Section One

The Sports Betting Marketplace

*In handicapping it's a cardinal sin
to assume you always should win.
Take your losses in stride
and like the ongoing tide
what ebbs out will inevitably flood in.*

1
The Winning Handicapper

The Professional's Example

Most handicappers who wager on football do so with the intention or dream of discovering the key to a hidden cache of wealth. I harbored dreams of wealth through gambling since I was in my mid-twenties. It was at this time that I first became impressed and enthralled with the world of gambling. This came as a result of my first visit to Nevada and its enticing casinos. I found myself dreaming of one day going to Reno armed with a system, breaking the bank and living a life of luxury and enjoyment. I spent countless hours with pen, pencil, pad, dice and other paraphernalia in order to to come up with *the system,* as millions of óthers had done before me.

I began my search for the winning system by acquiring several pairs of official dice. I then constructed a makeshift craps table with a corrugated backboard in order to obtain as many random occurrences as possible. I proceeded to throw the dice and record in sequence every number that came up. I did this over several weeks and recorded over 50,000 numbers in a ledger.

My next step took several weeks or maybe months. I tried to uncover some pattern in my records that would produce a winning system. I tried dozens of different possibilities for selecting numbers. I looked for patterns of sevens coming up. No matter what I tried, I always came up with approximately one seven in six rolls. I tried patterns for other bets (craps, elevens, the field), but always with the same disappointing results.

The results of my efforts convinced me of one thing: Defeating the casinos and walking away with all the cash was an illusion. I made several trips to Reno in order to test my systems against the realities of the casino environment. I never attained much success, mostly because I always had a limited bankroll. I did, however, win moderately most of the time, which kept my dream alive. Like most dreams, my fantasy was eventually shelved in the face of more important and realistic considerations, though it never quite died.

Some thirty years later, I moved to Las Vegas for reasons unrelated to gambling. The hopeful dream, dormant since my youth, was awakened when I stumbled into my first sports book. It wasn't long before I became intrigued with betting a few dollars on an occasional parlay card during the football season. Soon I was trying to find a way to beat the game.

Gradually I began to understand the concept of in-depth handicapping. As a consequence, I read, studied and became associated with several people in sports betting and, in 1980, found myself involved in the sports advisory business. Since then I have met, read about, hired, fired, listened to and observed more sports handicappers than just about anyone I know.

If there was but one quality by which I was allowed to judge any handicapper, it would unquestionably be his talent at weighing the factors he employs. Proper weighing is where the true art of handicapping lies. This is the art that separates the consistent winners from the perennial losers. If you ever wish to be a successful handicapper, you'd better learn how to establish relative value on those factors you consider when handicapping a game.

Never lose sight of the value of weight. If you possess the basic talent, or are an artist at weighing the factors and prognosticating from your assessments, then you will find yourself rapidly becoming more successful as you gain experience. You'll become known as everything from lucky, to a professional, to a genius.

While it is true that this process of weighing is of utmost importance to a handicapper's success, it is difficult to get inside a handicapper's head to see what factors he is considering and what weight he is giving to the various factors. Indeed, the handicapper himself may not be consciously aware of how he weighs the factors. A handicapper's quality must be judged primarily by his consistency.

Consistency is more than running hot and cold or even hot and lukewarm. It's producing a steady flow of more winners than losers. It's two or three good days, a bad day, and a couple of mediocre days, over and over again. More importantly, it's a winning season every season. Consistency identifies the true professional. The winning handicapper usually will make a cautious start at the onset of a new season and gain momentum throughout the season. The season will be concluded with a strong finish in the playoffs, not unlike a horse being paced throughout a race and then pulling away in the stretch. This is an exhibition of true class.

X The real professional is able to identify the most important factors, properly weigh them, and change his opinion in light of late information and line changes when necessary. Most of all, he is able to understand basic probability so that he avoids radical changes in his approach when he is in the inevitable losing streak. Overadjustment, overcompensation and excessive factor fiddling can transform a good handicapping program in a slump into a disaster. This overadjustment syndrome, which entraps many bettors, is not unlike the baseball player in a batting slump. The hitter becomes confused, starts making changes and adjustments which have no relation to his performance when he was hitting. Not until he accepts the slump as a manifestation of the laws of chance does he revert to his usual hitting tactics and come out of the slump.

What, then, can we learn from the professional's example? Above all, stick with what works for you, even in the hard times. Don't panic or press. Adjust only when there's no pressure and you are confident that the adjustment is sound.

In this book, I have tried to give the player sufficient information regarding the realities of sports betting and the techniques of handicapping so the reader can begin on his trek to betting profits. What is required on the reader's part is a commitment to carefully read this book and pursue his success in the sports betting marketplace as he would success in any other endeavor.

How to Become a Loser-Suggestion #1

Put only a little effort into becoming a handicapper. Chances are that a limited application of handicapping principles will play into the linesmaker's hands. The linesmaker knows the same information, making his job easier. Don't take the easy way out and flip a coin, throw darts or guess. These ways you're likely to lose only the vigorish, taking you much longer to lose your whole bankroll. Losing slowly lacks the anxiety and the letdowns so important to the enjoyment of losing.

Sports Betting

2

Past, Present and Future

Millons of dollars are wagered every weekend during the football season. Where did this betting craze begin? What factors have led to its growth and what will be its future?

According to Sonny Reizner, manager of the Castaways' Hole in the Wall Sports Book, sports betting in the United States began in the baseball parks shortly after World War I. Gradually it became a part of all major league baseball parks, in a section known as "right field."

Right field was where all the gamblers congregated. Frequenting right field were fans, handicappers, bookies, sportswriters and anyone else willing to back his opinion with his cash. Bets were mostly "one on one" and the money changed hands faster than at a street corner craps game. Bookmakers would ply their trade right at the ballpark. They would casually make up odds which were distributed to those interested. Bets were made on the outcome of the next pitch, the next hitter, the next inning and every other conceivable proposition.

An interesting side note, which Sonny relayed to me laughingly, was the strategically-placed signs in the grandstand areas of the park that stated "NO GAMBLING ALLOWED." What was funny was that this is where the gamblers would meet, making the signs a joke. During the Great Depression, though seats were cheap at the ballparks, attendance might be as low as 1000 or 1500 a game. The gambling crowd increased the attendance by 500 or 1000, accounting for a large percentage of the gross receipts. For this reason, gambling was overlooked, while the signs served to protect the ballpark management.

Baseball was the biggest gambling sport right up to the 1950s. Basketball was a distant second and hockey was even further back in third. Prior to World War II, football was not considered much of a gambler's sport and action on it was limited.

After World War II, around 1945, football started to become more popular as a betting proposition. A few small sports books opened up in downtown Las Vegas. Also, at about the same time, bookies in the larger metropolitan areas began taking more and more action on professional and college games. The main difficulty which inhibited a rapid increase in betting was the lack of a correct, uniform odds line. If a team was two or three touchdowns better than another, the odds might be 8-5 or 9-5 on the favorite.

Sonny told me it was the pointspread concept, which came into existence over thirty years ago, which really put football betting into high gear. A man named Ed Curd was very much responsible for implementing the pointspread, though no one seems to know where and by whom it was originated. The pointspread gave the bookmakers the tool they needed to entice bettors to bet on both sides when one team was heavily favored. The pointspread concept will be covered in more depth in Chapter 3.

The next big boon to football betting was television. As the NFL grew and solidified as an organization with the support of the media, the volume of betting increased exponentially. Today there are approximately 30 licensed sports books in Nevada, most in Las Vegas. On a fall weekend, during the height of the college and NFL seasons, these sports books accept millions of dollars in action. But Las Vegas is only a small part of the sports betting marketplace. There are an estimated 100,000 private (illegal) bookies, located throughout the country, who take action on sports. The amount of money changing hands is estimated to be $50 billion a year.

Both the National Football League and the United States Football League appear strong in the mid-1980s. I predict the NFL could consist of 40 franchises by the end of the century and the USFL could contain 30. The USFL has more than the hope of survival. It has financial support sufficient to see itself though its formative years. If the USFL can gain the support of television and the press, increase its quality and establish fans, it will not only survive, but will prosper.

This continued and increasing strength of the professional football leagues will be brought on by increased public interest, manifested in increased betting volume. I predict that by the middle-1990s there will be more than a half-trillion dollars per year wagered on professional sports. I predict that accompanying this increase in wagering volume will be a move to legalize sports betting in most states, following the precedent already established in Nevada. Where else might the government find such an activity of such universal interest that they can readily tax? Properly promoted and given enough convenience, sports betting will soon outdistance all other forms of government-sanctioned gambling. When the proper formula is discovered, legal bookmaking will be commonplace and illegal bookmakers will find it difficult to operate. By diverting some of the new tax money resulting from legalized sports gambling and commiting it to the enforcement of gambling laws, the number of illegal bookmakers can be substantially reduced.

How to Become a Loser-Suggestion #2

Do not analyze the odds you are playing against or concern yourself with the costs of a sports service. You might be able to reduce these costs if you became aware of them and inadvertently become a winner. The less you know, the more likely you'll end up a loser. Try to emulate the craps-playing high roller who keeps tossing his chips to the dealers, giving the casino an even higher edge. Buy three or four services and play their consensus of losers. Play against 12–to–10 odds if your bookmaker asks. Using these suggestions, you can insure that you will need 60% winners just to break even.

3

The Propositions

The Pointspread, Parlays, Teasers and Totals

The sports bettor is offered several different possibilities when he decides to wager on a sporting event. Here we will discuss and explain the pointspread, parlays, teasers and totals wagers. The player must decide when a particular proposition is appropriate for a situation and when it should be passed.

The Pointspread

If there has ever been a concept incorporated into the gambling industry which supersedes the impact of pari-mutuel betting, it is the introduction of the pointspread into sports wagering. The cleverness of this device can be best measured by the billions of dollars that change hands each year during the football season.

Gerald Strine and Neil Isaacs in *Covering the Spread* suggest the use of the pointspread concept began in Minneapolis in the late-1920s or early-1930s; however, it did not become nationally popular until after World War II.

Football teams are seldom viewed by the public as equal in strength, ability, talent and coaching. At times, the disparity between opposing teams is so great, especially in college sports, that creating odds that would equalize the teams (and assure equal betting action on both teams) would be extremely difficult. Something was needed to create an equal chance for both teams, even in a mismatched contest. The pointspread concept completely satisfied this need. Nothing since the advent of horse racing, including casino gaming, can compare with the general interest, participation and amount of money wagered on sporting events. This is especially true of professional football, which tops the action by far.

With the pointspread factored in, the outcome of one's wager on a football game is rarely decided until the last minutes and, in a large percentage of these, not until the final seconds. It doesn't matter who wins or loses the game. The game within the game is which team will beat the spread.

The true importance of laying or getting points on a wager lies in its simplicity. Assuming reasonable parity, which exists in most college conferences and especially in professional sports, the pointspread device makes almost every conceivable match-up a potential wagering opportunity. With his opinion in the form of a betting number, the linesmaker can induce thousands of individuals to wager millions of dollars on a nationally-televised football game. When the linesmaker releases a number on a game, it might be compared to someone tossing a snowball from the top of a mountain that ends up as an avalanche in a matter of seconds.

Let's take a look at some of the mechanics of the pointspread and see how these relate to its function and the results of the game they represent.

The pointspread is a number chosen by the linesmaker to create an equal division of public opinion, in terms of money wagered. The number signifies how many points the team chosen as the "favorite" will beat the "underdog." If the pointspread were -3 points on the favorite, that team would have to win by more than three points for the bettor on the favorite to collect on his wager. Conversely, the underdog ("dog") would be $+3$ points, meaning the team may lose the game by one or two points and the bettor still wins the wager. If the favorite wins by exactly three points, the wager would be considered a tie (a "push" in gambling parlance) and the bet would be called off.

A modification of the original concept is the half point, the origin of which I've been unable to trace. This represents the adding or subtracting a half point from the whole number. For example, -3 points may be changed to -2½ or -3½ . The half point, commonly referred to as "the hook," was devised to eliminate pushes, converting them into wins or losses. The modification and introduction of the half point, however, does a lot more than eliminate pushes. To the linesmaker or bookmaker, the movement of a line up or down by ½ point can be critical in the following ways:

1. It may be an indicator as to which team is getting the most betting action.

2. It can provide an inducement or detraction for the bettor, inviting him to bet on one side or the other.

3. It can have crucial impact on the betting outcome of certain games, especially when the pointspread is divisible by three or seven. Similarly, it can be important when the pointspread is -1 or -1½.

4. When the linesmaker or bookmaker moves the line a full point or more at a time, the half-point option ignored serves to disclose a major change in intelligence on the game in question.

There are other subtleties of the pointspread but I will go into these in more detail in the chapter covering line analysis. Let me remind you that if you are, or wish to become a sports bettor, it doesn't matter which team wins the game. The only question you'll want to concern yourself with is, "Who will beat the spread?"

Parlays

It is frequently said that parlays, where the winnings from one bet are automatically re-bet on another bet or series of bets, are a bad wager and should be avoided by the intelligent sports bettor. Mathematicians claim the odds on parlays are less favorable than the eleven-to-ten proposition available when making a straight bet. That is true; they are less favorable in most cases. However, I will demonstrate in this chapter that there are instances when betting parlays can be favorable to the player.

Before the player can decide whether parlays can be useful to him in his struggle to beat the bookmaker, he must know what the true odds are and what a player sacrifices when he makes a two- or three-team parlay play at the standard bookie odds. I will also explain when such a proposition is appropriate and how less risk for a larger gain can be justified when one has a limited bankroll or when other factors (money management, pointspread odds and opportunity) come into play.

Let's consider first the two-team parlay. Say I wish to place a wager of $110 to win $100 on team A in game one. (This is the usual situation on a one-game proposition and requires 52.38% winners to break even.) Upon winning game one, I cash in my ticket and receive $210 from the cashier, which I immediately bet on team B in game two. If and when I win this bet, I go back to the cashier and collect $400.91, my total payoff for winning both bets. When I subtract my original investment of $110, I will have realized a profit of $290.91.

What I really did was parlay the winnings of my first bet into the second. The odds never changed, remaining 11 to 10 in each case. No matter what you call it, I've made a two-team parlay without sacrificing any additional edge. There is only one catch to making the above parlay: You must pick two games that are not being played simultaneously. Furthermore, the first game must be concluded and won before the second game starts, giving you time to wager before the bookmaker stops accepting action on the game.

Take the two-team parlay ticket that pays 13 to 5 at most sports books in Las Vegas. To keep it simple, I will use the same numbers as mentioned earlier. If you were to buy a two-team parlay ticket at 13 to 5 and wagered $110, you would get back a profit of $286 ($13×22).

Now you can compare the two parlays. The profit from the first parlay ticket was $4.91 greater than the second ticket. How does this affect the player's break-even point? We have already indicated that the player must hit 52.38% on his plays to break even on an 11 to 10 proposition, and we will discuss this at greater length in the next chapter. With the 13 to 5 parlay, we would need to hit 52.70% winners to break even. The bookie would pay out one out of four parlays and collect his 5% edge.

Let's look at a three-team parlay figured both ways. As we have already discovered, if we bet $110 to win $100, take the $210 returned and bet it on a second play, the payoff comes to $400.91. If we wager that $400.91 on a third play, we will win an additional $364.46. Our total return will be $400.91+$364.46 or $765.37. If we should bet the same initial amount, $110, on a parlay ticket at 6-1, we would be paid $660 in winnings, plus our investment of $110, for a total of $770. *We actually would make $4.63 more on the parlay ticket than on the 11-to-10 proposition.* What impact does this have on our break-even percentage? We would only need to hit 52.28% winners to break even betting three-team parlays.

Forget all parlays of four games or more. The odds get increasingly worse as you add more games. If you play parlays, play two- or three-teamers, preferably the three-teamers.

Now that the odds have been explained, under what conditions should a player invest in a parlay? Obviously, if two teams are playing simultaneously and your handicapping points them out as solid plays, you should go ahead and play the parlay ticket at 13 to 5. This is particularly true if you have limited capital to risk. Another instance in which it is sensible to play a parlay is when you fear the pointspread on the second game will move against you before the first game is completed. A half-point move against you is worth approximately 2% to the bookie. In this case, you are better off playing the 13 to 5 parlay.

If you decide a parlay is appropriate, your money management guidelines must be adjusted. You will see later that 2% of your bankroll is a comfortable, conservative play when making several plays simultaneously. If one's bankroll was $5000, then an optimum regular play might be 4% or $200. Since your chances of winning both games in a parlay are one in four instead of one in two, you should reduce your play by half, which amounts to 2% or $100 of a $5000 bankroll.

* * *

Teasers

Teasers are another breed of parlay. A teaser is a proposition where the bettor may move a pointspread a given number of points in his favor on two or more games, provided he plays the games together in a parlay. For example, Team A may be -7 and Team B may be -3. When coupled together in a six-point teaser, you move the line on Team A to -1 and Team B to +3. Of course, the odds are reduced substantially. Two team, six-point teasers pay even money compared to the straight two team parlay which pays 13 to 5. The three team, six-point teasers return 9 to 5 instead of the 6 to 1 on a straight parlay.

In Las Vegas, there are six-, seven-, and 10-point teasers. The greater the number of points teased, the worse the odds become.

The odds on teasers are not subject to pure mathematics, as are straight parlays. If one had the time and patience to make the thousands of calculations necessary, he could determine if any pointspread numbers show a high percentage of winners in teasers.

Let's take a hypothetical situation. In reviewing the records, we discover certain match-ups almost always finish within two, three or four points of the pointspread. This might be due to the parity of the teams, coaching methods or other factors. You might look for these situations to play. Needless to say, teasers require a lot of work in order to find good plays. Generally, they are a questionable bet. I do play a few, when my handicapping indicates they are a good risk. Unless you have done your homework on this proposition, however, you are better off concentrating on other types of wagers.

The Totals Wager

There is no doubt that the bookies believe they have a solid handle on the pointspread, proof of which is the relatively large bets they'll accept, especially on professional football. If the pointspread is the security blanket for bookmakers, then totals (over/under) betting is their nemesis.

In the totals proposition, the bookmaker establishes a number for the total score in a game (both teams) and the player chooses to wager that the actual score will go over or under the posted score. Totals betting apparently was begun about 1963 in Las Vegas by Bill Dark, a very wise player and sports book operator. It began as a gimmick, an inducement for bettors to drive the 3-5 miles to visit Bill's book, the Del Mar Race and Sports Club. Bill reasoned that he needed an idea to draw the bettors in. He knew he could come up with a mean number to represent the final score of a game, based on the league average and certain other relevant handicapping factors.

For several years Bill was about the only sports book in Las Vegas who risked his bankroll on the totals proposition. Eventually a few other sports books in and around Las Vegas began to post totals numbers on selected games. The idea finally broke out of the confines of Las Vegas and bookmakers around the country began obtaining a totals line. By 1980, the concept was pretty much entrenched as a standard betting proposition in all but a few isolated areas of the country. Speaking of those isolated areas, it seems that in some populated areas there is a hierarchy of bookmakers, who "lay off" their action to bookmakers higher in the system. Apparently, totals betting is looked on as too risky because of the weather and late injury factor. Late-breaking information can make the "lay off" system inoperative. This scenario represents my opinion, but I can't come up with any other reason why no bookie in Chicago, Pittsburgh and some other Eastern cities will accept a totals bet.

Demand for totals betting among players continues to increase and, in due time, the bookies will find protection from the sharp players. One edge some bookies have already taken is to offer 6 to 5 odds and thus increase the vigorish from 4.55% to 8.33%. Granted, on a 50-50 proposition, this is a lot of "juice" to overcome. From a handicapping and playing viewpoint, I feel at least as confident betting selected totals at 6 to 5 as I do betting pointspread selections at 11 to 10. Most books limit bets on the totals proposition to a fraction of what they will accept on pointspread wagers.

How to Become a Loser-Suggestion #3

Deal only with one bookie. Be sure to let him know everything about you and how you play so he can create additional edges for himself. Don't ask for any favors, such as a half point. He may break down in a weak moment, fear the loss of your patronage and accidentally deal you a winning line. If you found yourself beating your "man," he'll be forced to cut you off or limit your action, leaving you no place to lose.

The Bettor's Adversary

"Wise Guys," Linesmaker or Bookmaker?

Who is the bettor's adversary when he places a football bet? This is not a simple question. To answer it, we must consider the individuals who interact with the bettor directly or affect the pointspread number the bettor faces. Let's outline the process that occurs before the bookmaker offers the odds or pointspread to his clients.

First, there is the linesmaker. He determines what number will most likely attract equal betting on both sides of a game. Once this number has been initially determined, it is then released as an "outlaw" line to a select few bettors, mostly in Las Vegas, who express their opinion of this line with their bets. This occurs on Sunday night within a few hours of the conclusion of the last pro game played that day.

These "outlaw" line players are considered to be among the sharpest handicappers in the country. They are, in sports betting parlance, the "wise guys," those whose opinions are most highly regarded by the linesmaker. Once the bets have been made, the lines are adjusted, so they reflect, not only the linesmaker's opinion, but the collective opinion of some of the sharpest bettors in existence.

On Monday morning, the opening line is released to the public via a network of bookies throughout the United States. Very few of these bookies, however, will accept any betting action (wagers) into these lines early in the week. Some sports books will take limited action against the opening line. This early action immediately reflects the opinions of some of the sharpest public players. These bettors give the linesmaker additional information as to public opinion, giving rise to further line adjustments, which will more accurately reflect the general public's betting later in the week.

By the time most bookmakers release a betting line to the majority of their clients, it has already been worked over by some of the smartest and heaviest action in the country. The system described virtually guarantees a 50/50 split in public opinion on a nationwide basis.

Sometimes mistakes are made. Injuries, weather and other conditions can affect the odds by game time. But the linesmaker and bookies can absorb this small percentage of disfavor by adjusting the line for their late action. These mistakes, however, can be profitable for the sharp players, who act quickly before the line moves.

I opened this chapter by asking who the player's adversary might be. Is he the linesmaker, the wise guys who bet into the outlaw and early lines, or the local bookie who takes the player's action? Obviously, they all represent the opposition to the average player. It is the bookie, however, who has the final say, representing all the others who affect the line. Is the inanimate betting line itself the real opponent of the player, with the bookmaker just the representative, the end of the process? But it is the bookmaker who makes the final and individual line adjustments which he offers to his clients. The question remains—who is the player's real adversary? The correct answer has to be the line as an entity in itself, which is represented by the linesmaker, the sharp players, quality handicappers and the bookies, all working collectively to siphon off their percentages of the billions of dollars that change hands each year.

The Bookmaker

Let's examine the sports bookie and see if we can classify him. Though the fluctuating betting line is the player's real adversary, it is personified in the bookmaker(s) with whom the player deals. The bookmaker is, above all, a businessman. He must make a profit to stay in business.

The bookmaker is not much different from a stockbroker who makes a commission on each of his client's transactions. The more shares the stockbroker buys and sells, the more money he makes. With the bookmaker, the more action he accepts from his clients, the more vigorish ("juice") he realizes. It is here where the analogy ends. While the stockbroker makes money every time a transaction is completed, the bookmaker only makes a guaranteed profit when he has balanced action on a proposition. Additionally, bookmakers outside Nevada face additional hurdles. Because bookmaking is illegal, the bookmaker can be arrested or forced to pay protection money. He can also get "stiffed" (not paid) by his clients who bet more than they can afford and renege on their losses.

The bookie's primary advantage is that he deals an 11-to-10 proposition to his clients. The bookie makes you put up $11 to win $10. Under these conditions, he only needs to hit 47.62% winners on the total action he accepts to break even, while the players must hit 52.38% before they realize any profit. If the bookie gets equal action on both sides of a game, he will lock in a profit of 4.55% on his total action. In reality this is not exactly what happens. A large percentage of bookmakers have too few clients to assure balanced books. Even with a large clientele, most of the action will be on a few of the many available plays and this action might be heavy on one side of those games. In other words, bookies seldom, if ever, have balanced action on every game they deal. The bookie expects 50% of all money wagered to be on the winning side and 50% on the losing side *in the long run,* but he is generally not averse to creating additional hidden edges.

What are these additional edges that the bookie can use to increase his percentage from 4.55% to as much as 10% or 15%? (Incidentally, by mentioning these edges, I am in no way condemning bookies in general. I am trying to make the bettor more aware of the bookies' actions and their own options.)

1. The bookie may move the points in his favor. Though this might better balance his books, it is more often done because the direction of the move indicates the winning side. If you always bet into a sharp football line, there is a good probability you will be flipping a coin at best, unless you're an exceptionally good handicapper or are privy to the same information available to those who win.

2. The bookie may insist you play into greater negative odds, say 12 to 10, more commonly known as 6 to 5. This move increases the bookmaker's edge from 4.55% to approximately 8.33%, which means the player's break-even point moves from 52.38% to 54.55%.

3. It has been estimated that a half-point move on every game can favor the mover as much as 2.5%. If the linesmaker or bookie responsible is right four out of five times (and he usually is), he's picked up an additional two percentage points.

4. The bookie may take pushes, which is common in totals (over/under) betting. If one game out of 40 lands on the number,

a realistic assessment, the bookie wins both sides 2.5% of the time, for another 5% edge.

5. The bookie can middle his clients on total bets by making them play over one number and under another. For example, he could offer over 42 and under 40. If the total score lands on 40, he pushes the under and wins the over. If it lands on 42, he pushes the over and wins the under. If the total ends up 41, a 20-1 shot, he's middled all his clients and won both sides of that game's total bet. The bookie has eliminated the real push and picked up another hidden 5% edge.

6. The bookie can circle a game, therefore limiting his action on that game. Through use of this device, he can keep clients from placing large bets early on one number and late on another number, possibly getting middled and endangering his bankroll. Late information, reflecting changed conditions, weather or injuries may change the pointspread or totals line; to combat this tendency, the bookie can circle a game or take it off the board completely.

7. The bookie may peg your playing habits and create another edge for himself. Let's say he discovers your play is represented by 80% favorites. All the bookie must do to gain a few percentage points in his favor is to move all the favorites a half point or, daringly, a full point. The bookie will have the best of it four out of five times.

There are many more edges an enterprising bookie can create for himself, but the ones I cover here are the major ones. These additional edges can devastate a player's bankroll. A player able to hit 60% against a good Vegas line at 11 to 10 would be lucky to break even playing the same games against his local bookie on the bookie's terms.

You now know some of the many prerogatives and options at your bookie's disposal in his efforts to beat you. What can you, the player, do to overcome some or all of the odds stacked against you?

Here are some options for the player to exercise, to keep his bookie in check and to avoid the pitfalls that entrap the majority of players.

1. Know what the current adjusted betting line is before you contact your bookie. Have him run down his line before you make your plays. If possible, tell him you'll get back to him in a few minutes, as soon as you make your final selections. This gives you the opportunity to check his line against another line. You might reconsider your plays where the lines differ substantially. This procedure is especially effective when you can get lines from two, three or more books.

2. If you handicap a play and are unable to get reasonable odds, you are better off telling your bookie his numbers are off and pass. If he has been trying to take advantage of you, he will "clean up" his act, especially if he thinks he is losing valuable business.

3. Never be afraid to ask your bookie for a half point or a better money line if you feel he's off the mark. Tell him you'll give him the play at a certain number. If he says no, pass a few times. He'll eventually come around, especially if he thinks you're taking your business elsewhere.

4. If your bookie will only deal totals at 6 to 5 odds, try and get an extra half point to cover the extra vigorish.

5. Don't play totals with a bookie who takes pushes, unless his totals are half-point totals and coincide with the national line.

6. Don't play football totals against a bookie who makes you play over one number and under another, both being a point higher or lower than the "correct" number. An exception to this occurs when the number the bookie is dealing, high or low, is as good or better than the number you were already considering going over or under.

In the final analysis, the bookie is your true adversary. If you are unsure of what you are doing in choosing your plays and spots, he will beat you every time. If, instead, you learn to be a smart player, you may be able to keep your bookie accepting your action and paying off your winners, with the expectation that your "luck" will change and he will get even.

When it comes to handicapping football, don't forget to handicap your bookmaker. He's one factor that carries a lot of weight in your win/loss expectation.

How to Become a Loser-Suggestion #4

If you should find a good handicapping or sports advisory service, be sure to drop them at the first indication of losing. Find a loser who's starting to win. Nobody wins or loses all the time. The best way to assure losing with sports advisory services is to jump from one to another. Your fears and anxieties are bound to direct you to more losers than winners.

5

Probability

Odds and Their Ends

All professional, as well as the majority of amateur gamblers, have some understanding of the laws of probability, even though they many not know the exact definition or formulae behind this understanding. However, the more one learns about mathematical probability, the more accurately and confidently the player can make decisions that have a direct effect on his handicapping and gambling results. Ridding oneself of belief in luck, hope and Santa Claus will allow the gambler to have more realistic expectations and consequently help him develop better money management habits. This is by far the most important step a successful gambler must make. Understanding and applying the laws of probability when gambling is absolutely essential to becoming a true winner.

I will now present six of the most important postulates relevant to successful sports betting. Any gambler who hopes to become a winner should adhere to these guidelines.

1. If a sports bettor has a better than break-even percentage going for him, the probability of him ending up a winner is in direct proportion to the number of plays he makes. In other words, your chances of winning are greater when playing 1000 games than when playing 100 games, assuming the same win/loss expectancy. Putting it another way, your money is safer betting $100 on ten separate games than $1000 on one game at the same ex-

pectancy. Since the laws of probability are more accurately represented as the number of trials increases, one protects himself best by making a greater number of smaller bets.

2. Even with a high win percentage, a result of good handicapping, the player can't avoid losing streaks. The successful gambler plans for such contingencies and avoids a "bust out." Let's suppose you started with a bankroll of $1000 and decided to play $200 a game. It would take only five net losers, not including the juice, to lose your entire bankroll. Obviously, you should play a smaller amount on each play if you wish to increase the safety factor. Exercise conservatism and you'll have more fun, either taking longer to lose it all or, hopefully, win at a steadier, more certain pace.

3. The frequency and length of winning and losing streaks vary in direct proportion to your win percentage. Even in a season with 60% winners, you could still experience extended losing streaks. All that a higher win percentage predicts is that you can expect shorter and less frequent losing streaks. The problem with most bettors is they will not accept this fact. They either change sports services frequently when a losing streak occurs or overadjust and make things worse.

4. In sports betting, what has happened in the past will most likely continue to happen in the future only if the conditions which created the results remain approximately the same. This postulate is most important. The components of a team are in constant flux. In professional sports, franchises change hands and relocate; coaches get fired and hired; players retire or are traded; rules change. In college sports, one can add the rapid turnover of first-string players due to graduation. Don't expect a trend to continue when one or more conditions change. Be extremely careful when many changes occur in a short period of time. In such a case, you will be dealing with an entirely new group of factors and variables.

5. Find and utilize to your advantage a situation in conflict with the laws of probability. When properly understood, this can produce some of the best betting propositions available. Let me provide some examples of this postulate in action. In pro football, nearly half of all games played will total scores less than 30 points or over 52 points. The linesmaker, however, cannot put up a 60 or 20 on a game because it would encourage one-sided action. A good handicapper can find solid plays by looking for these situations.

6. If the player adheres to a mathematically-sound money management program, he need only surpass the break-even percentage for that proposition to win. You could hit 65% winners and still end up a loser if you fail in the money management department. Erratic betting, varying the size of one's bet, can only be justified if higher bet sizes are related to higher percentage performance. It might be mathematically sound and consistent with the laws of probability to make different size bets, but a double play should be on a game with 5% to 10% greater chance of winning. Don't guess. Keep records and develop criteria for classification and establish an appropriate share of the bankroll for each classification.

The postulates mentioned here are based on pure mathematics. Good handicapping will tell you when you should deviate from these principles.

How to Become a Loser-Suggestion #5

Don't study or become familiar with the laws of probability. Avoid acquiring any knowledge of chance, probability or mathematics. Knowing these laws, you would play cautiously and wisely, almost guaranteeing that you'd become a winner.

6

Investor or Gambler?

A "Bottom-Line" Analysis

Sports betting can be a very good form of investment. In many ways, as you will see, it can be considered equal to or better than the stock market, where millions of people invest billions of dollars each year. Let's consider some of the factors that would normally be considered by an individual with money to invest.

Doubling Your Bankroll

When it comes to making money in the stock market, an investor can expect to turn over his investment portfolio no faster than once every two or three years. Obviously, one would need a lot of money invested in securities to make a living from such profits or to increase his wealth quickly. Only the big manipulators and wise guys in the market know how to convert the dynamics of the Exchange into riches for themselves.

The sports gambler who is a professional or engages the services of professionals, on the other hand, can double his investment capital several times each year. It is not impossible for a sports bettor with a $10,000 bankroll to indulge in $1 million of action a year at a profit of 8% to 10% of that million dollars. That amounts to $80,000–$100,000 of profits yearly.

Ups and Downs

The stock market is subject to many fluctuations and unpredictable circumstances. Every ripple in the economy, caused by political, social or seasonal problems or just rumors can affect the market in a matter of weeks, days or hours. Getting in and out at the right time is crucial to success.

The sports betting market is also subject to many variables and unpredictable contingencies. Like the stock market, those who know the most and are on top of what is pertinent or relevant profit. One must always be alert and ready to make a profitable transaction at the right time.

Costs and Fees

When working with a stockbroker, the investor pays a fee to the broker for each transaction the broker makes in his behalf. Unless the investor stipulates definite buy or sell points, he could become the victim of "churning," where many transactions are executed by the broker to generate commissions. It should be pointed out that the broker who generates commissions makes money regardless of the fate of the investor's money.

An investor with limited knowledge may instead contract with a portfolio manager. The portfolio manager works on a profit-sharing basis and there is no way his interests can conflict with the investor's.

The sports gambler pays a commission to the bookmaker on every wager he makes. If he pays for sports advice, he can be put in the same situation as the stock market investor. There are instances where the sports service can profit when the gambler loses. The only way this would not be the case is when the service is paid out of profits or net units won. This is a balanced and equitable deal. However, a service may still manipulate the plays, either to protect accumulated net units won or to try to erase an accumulated net loss. If you pay a flat fee, make sure the service has proven credentials and charges fees that are reasonable considering your total action. A reasonable fee would be in the range of 1%–2% of the total action.

Morality

Do not confuse the morality of gambling on sports with that of gambling on the stock market. If one is immoral, so is the other. Because one is more socially acceptable does not change this basic fact. For each person's gain, one or more individuals must lose. The rationalization that one is productive and the other is non-productive is open to argument. The stock market player may contend that his money helps develop the general economy and create jobs. This is true, but this is not the investor's purpose. His real purpose is by no means altruistic.

Many readers probably will not consider gambling as an investment. These individuals would rather handicap for fun or engage in outright gambling, contending that gambling with a certainty of winning is less exciting. Me? I find it much more exciting and pleasurable to know I'll end up a winner, having met the challenge and succeeded.

How to Become a Loser-Suggestion #6

Suppose you've been lucky enough to have a losing week and Monday Night Football is coming up. Try and bail yourself out by putting your whole week's losses on the Monday game. Even if you win the Monday game 50% of the time, think of the fun you'll have being a double loser the other Monday nights and how many times you'll have to sweat to pay the "man" on Tuesday? This kind of high and low in your otherwise dull life can be really exciting.

7

Sports Services

Touts and Louts

The various trade publications of the sports betting industry are inundated with advertisements for sports services, organizations willing to sell you betting advice for a price. To my knowledge these publications do not require verification of claims made by advertisers. It seems that the publications in question want only the sports service's money. Most will print whatever you want as long as you pay. Similar claims are made through the mails, to anyone who has answered a sports service ad or subscribed to a sports betting publication.

One of the problems with many sports bettors is they are willing to pay hundreds or thousands of dollars for advice from sports services without checking out the validity of the claims and the quality of the advice they are purchasing. Many of these individuals are astute businessmen who wouldn't think of making a business decision without checking it out first from every conceivable angle. They protect themselves by insuring their homes and valuables. Yet they are ready to believe any lies the gimmick-oriented sports service will tell them.

Gimmicks

What are some of the more common gimmicks used by the majority of sports services intent on getting the customer's money without necessarily producing winners?

Locks

I guess the word lock has been used more than any other to convince the naive sports gambler to give his money to self-proclaimed geniuses. When the sports service uses the word lock, they are stating that the game cannot lose. They have found that if they say it loud enough and print it bold enough, a certain percentage of players will believe them. They have also found that the more money they ask for their lock, the easier it is to sell.

The lock concept preys upon the bettor who has been losing and wants to recoup quickly. This kind of player is looking for the miracle that will bail him out. In this quest for a miracle, the bettor loses sight of reality. Always keep in mind that a play is a play. It can lose or win. The "expert" with the lock is implying that he knows more than the linesmaker, the bookies, the wise guys, the players and the officials. Almost anything can happen in a football game and a turnover or bad punt can totally alter the course of a game.

Never forget that a lock is an even-money bet, minus the juice. It should be treated no different than any other play on a justifiable rating system. If the play is so good, why is the service selling it to you? For the price of a plane ticket, the seller could come to Las Vegas and clean up. The fact that none of these "locksmiths" ever do this should be cause for caution.

Double Dealing

Imagine a sports service that is not monitored by any reputable monitoring service. Let's suppose also that the sports service claims it wins 70% of its selections. With this hype to substantiate its offer, the service offers a 1000-star lock for a game next weekend and the cost to you is $150, $250 or even more.

If the sports service gets 500 people in its net, it is easily to calculate what they can realize. All they need do is deal half the customers one side of the game and the other half the other side. This guarantees 250 winners. Now the ante goes up. The next week the salesman talks with the winning clients and asks, "How did you like that big winner we gave you last week? I hope you got down big." If the price was $150 for the first game, the price may rise to $200 or $300 for the next release. The second week cuts the number of winners from 250 to 125 and continues until the final split.

No matter what week you lose, you'll end up a victim, disillusioned and broke, while the service has extracted thousands of dollars in fees with their scams.

The Lay-off Scam

The tout service offers you the so-called "can't lose" pick for $300, guaranteeing your money back if you lose. The service lays off $165 ($150, plus $15 vigorish) on the other side, leaving him $135. If you win, the service loses $165 to the bookmaker and profits $135. If you lose, the service collects $150 profit from his bookmaker and returns your $300. This accomplishes two things for the scam artists. They have gained your confidence. They also will be back for more easy money. It doesn't really matter whether the service picks 50% or 60% winners; at $150 a pick (assuming 50% winners), the service will do very well.

Returning More Than You Paid

"Pay me $300 for the game and I'll pay you $450 if it loses." Have you seen this one in sports publications? Here's how it works. The service gets perhaps 100 responses. They give 50 people one side and 50 people the other side. At $300 a pop, they take in $30,000. But they don't keep it all. They continue the scam, week in and week out, until their customers run out of cash. In the scenario described here, the 50 losers will receive $450 each, a total of $22,500, and the sports service pockets $7500.

Another version of the same scam has the service charging $50 a game and offering a pay back of $60 on losers. This scam can have you paying for net losers. Suppose you bought seven plays at $50 each. The service deals you three winners and four losers. They return you $240, leaving them a profit of $110 for one net loser. Seeing the check from the service for your losers can lead you to proclaim, "What an honest service!" You're right back the next week with $350 more. The service can't lose unless they come up with a 1-6 or 0-7 weekend. After a week or two, they think they have you and may suggest, "Just apply the $180 (for three losers) to your next week's fee of $350."

There are a number of other scams, but these provide you with a number of examples to consider.

Protecting Yourself

What can you do to protect yourself? There are several things you should know:

1. Be skeptical when anyone offers you a sure thing. If it sounds too good to be true, it probably is. Anyone who offers you a lock is insulting your intelligence.

cards net them many times the profit of a straight 11 to 10 bet. A five team parlay win pays a whopping 20–1. Forget that the odds of hitting one are 31–1. Let the other guys worry about that. If you think you can overcome the percentage, go ahead and play them all.

Monitoring Services

Limited at Best

While the preceding chapter on sports services hopefully served to alert the bettor to the hazards of dealing with some sports services, there are organizations that can protect the sports service client from the unscrupulous and direct him to those services with proven handicapping talent. These are known as monitoring services.

Monitoring services can protect the sports bettor from being ripped off by the bad guys. Unfortunately, monitoring services, quality or otherwise, are limited in their numbers. In this chapter we will examine two monitoring services, the American Association of Documented Sports Services (AADSS) and the now-defunct The Absolute Truth. I will also offer some suggestions, so organizations like these can better serve the bettor.

The AADSS

The AADSS conducts handicapping contests each year in the three major sports. Handicappers and sports services may enter these contests and demonstrate their skills. The association's newsletter, *Sports Service News*, is primarily concerned with the contests, their progress and results. The organization also monitors sports service releases and rating of plays.

The AADSS has tried many marketing approaches directed at the consumers of sports advisory services. Most of these approaches have been unremunerative, simply because the majority of sports bettors are not looking for insurance in their blind desire for winners. The average sports bettor, in his gambling behavior, is immature and unrealistic. For him to admit that he needs protection is equivalent to admitting there is no Santa Claus and that winning is not automatic for him.

As a result of this and other obstacles, the AADSS has had to use a back-door approach, although they are still seeking cost-effective marketing strategies for reaching current and potential sports service subscribers. At this time, they have let the sports services, who are both their contest clients and monitoring service clients, to financially support them.

Sports services and handicappers are enticed to enter the contests sponsored by the AADSS because they can use the standings and results of these contests in their advertising and promotional campaigns. Winning any handicapping contest offers the winner a tremendous advantage in a market hungry for winners. Additionally, by the simple act of entering, the sports service operator indicates his willingness to compete and expose his company's handicapping capabilities to the general public.

Each contestant pays a fee to enter the contest. As an entrant, he is given an imaginary bankroll of $10,000. He may bet up to 10% or $1000 (whichever is greater) on a selection. There is no limit to the number of plays that can be made in any day, as long as the total amount of imaginary money wagered does not exceed his bankroll, which is adjusted either daily or weekly. The official Las Vegas line is used as the standard betting line. Certain weekday afternoon games (and certain other games) are excluded from play due to logistical considerations.

While I think generally the AADSS provides a valuable service to the sports bettor, I do have several suggestions to make the contests better serve their intended purpose. First of all, restrict the contestant to a maximum bet of 5% of his adjusted bankroll, no more than 10 plays a day, and no more than 30% of the bankroll at risk at one time. This would be consistent with good money management and would restrain contestants from getting involved in a crapshoot with their "funny money" bankrolls. No reputable sports service would advise a client to bet his whole bankroll at once, an option open to any contestant in an AADSS contest.

In the first half of the 1982-83 AADSS NBA contest, I employed a very strict money management program that I sold to my clients. I did not deviate from this plan from the first to the last day of the contest. My base play was 2% of my running bankroll to the nearest $100 (a restriction of the contest) and my largest play was 6%, utilized only a couple of times. I finished fourth in the contest. Keep in mind that my competition was playing 10% of their bankroll on most of their plays. The winner, Jim Pettit, a close friend of mine and a quality handicapper, had as his goal winning the contest with a money management plan that was realistic yet aggressive enough to beat all but the luckiest crapshooter. It all went down to the last day when the crapshooter went broke and lost.

Another modification I would propose is to limit the size of one bet to a maximum of $2000, regardless of the cumulative bankroll. This would better match the real world of bookmaking and force the handicapper to demonstrate his skill with more net winners. Finally, I suggest the AADSS list the entire standings of all contestants with continued emphasis on the top entrants.

Although I would like to see such changes and reforms in the future, I am sympathetic to the financial welfare of the AADSS. The AADSS will likely not implement changes until the betting public is willing to support them, making it unnecessary to compromise on behalf of the sports services. Although the purpose of the AADSS is to serve the needs of the sports bettor, the sports services remain the main support of AADSS. The AADSS has tried repeatedly and at great expense to reach the sports betting market with their service, only to be ignored by the vast majority. When the AADSS, or some other enterprising organization, does find a way to induce sports bettors to buy protection against the scam artists, the sports betting industry as a whole will be the benefactor.

The Absolute Truth

Mr. Skipper Vessels of La Cross, Georgia, instituted a concept and publication called *The Absolute Truth* in the fall of 1982. This publication monitored cooperative sports services at no cost to them, compiling data on wins, losses, percentages, ratings of plays and unit profits or losses. The information was made available to sports bettors for a modest fee. The effort failed for several reasons. It was underfinanced and did not know how to convince and convert an indifferent market. Secondly, it did not know how to best market and price its product. Thirdly, it was understaffed and lacked the proper sales personnel to best present its product. Lastly, the 1982 NFL strike put Vessels' dream into limbo and scared off its financial backing. I hope someone picks up the pieces and puts together a well-conceived, practical publication like *The Absolute Truth*.

The Unmonitored Service

A sports service that is not monitored is not necessarily a bad one. Only the sports service in this case knows for sure. You would have to use your own judgement to discern the worth of such a service. The service may not wish to spend the money to be monitored, or feel that such an effort would be useless to their marketing strategies. There are other reasons as well for refusing to be monitored. The service may believe their selections are too valuable to be released to anyone other than a client. I would never buy this reasoning, though I can't fault their integrity by questioning their ego or their concepts of good business. The service also may not wish to reveal that they cannot win all the time. Lastly, they may simply be so indifferent that they just can't be bothered. If this is their attitude, what would their attitude be towards their customers?

Obviously, it would be easier for the sports bettor if all sports services were monitored by a reputable organization. The player must be especially careful whenever he deals with a service that is not monitored.

How to Become a Loser-Suggestion #8

Why fool around playing a lot of games? The old "safety in numbers" theory will drag out your losing and become boring. Bet all your money on the turn of a card or the bounce of a ball. Pick the best play on the card, the "lock of the century," and lay your whole bankroll on it. Why waste time going broke? If you're going to be a loser, do it in style. An alternative to the one big play approach is to bet several games at once, risking your entire bankroll each time you play. Why fool around when you might get rich in a hurry? The sports bettor who adopts the high roller's "let it ride" philosophy and continually tries to parlay his winnings will eventually make a few bad picks and attain the status of a full-fledged loser.

9

Have You Ever Wondered?

Questions For Answers

Why, with all the sports services, professional handicappers, bar room quarterbacks and others who claim to have the winners, do the vast majority of players lose and the bookies get rich? The answer is simple: It is extremely difficult to beat the betting line consistently.

Have you ever wondered why you can talk to two different handicappers and get a strong case for either side? Give me 20 games, 40 sides and 100 handicappers and I'll get a strong case to cover every play.

Have you ever wondered why a good handicapper can turn bad? If an individual can hit 57% in 1000 games, he's more than just good! However, in this effort, he might have a 65–70% streak of winners over 100 games and a losing streak with 45% winners over another 100 games. The laws of probabilty are erratic in the short run, but become more predictable in the long run. If a person consistently beats the game over a period of time, he's more than just lucky. Have you ever wondered why certain people are always lucky? Or is it just pure luck?

Have you ever wondered why your "man" is usually off ½ to a full point or more from the Las Vegas or "true" line? Maybe he has your action pegged. The bookmaker is not much different from a used car dealer in that you can negotiate with him. You don't have to play totally on the bookmaker's terms? Ask for a half point or pass. Let him think that your other "man" will give you a better deal. Remember, the bookmaker makes his money on his total action. As a businessman, he doesn't like to turn away paying customers. If you're a big enough player and get to your bookmaker early enough, you are in a better position to negotiate because the bookmaker has time to position himself for the heavy late action.

Have you ever wondered why the bigger sports services seem to be the ones that put out the most hype? How do you think they got big? When it comes to taking your money, these predators make your local bookie look like Saint Generosity. It seems that the more hype they expound, the more successful they become as a business. Haven't you also wondered why they never allow themselves to be monitored? Why don't they just claim they never lose and be done with upmanship? Don't you know it is just as easy to pick 100% winners as 80% winners after the fact?

Have you ever wondered why the self-acclaimed geniuses who advertise and proclaim to pick 70%, 80% or more winners don't just play the games themselves instead of trying to sell them to you? There's nothing wrong with a decent handicapper sharing his success for a few bucks but at 80% he would make exactly 58% profit on every dollar wagered. He'd double his money every two days! Have you ever believed these individuals to the point of giving them your money?

How to Become a Loser-Suggestion #9

There are many heartless, greedy charlatans and outright liars and thieves who abound on the tout side of the sports betting industry. These predators mercilessly prey upon the weaknesses of the sports bettor. Buy the services of those who make the most outrageous claims of success and promise you the most winners, locks and riches. Pay them what they ask and do exactly as instructed. By adherence to these guidelines, you'll be assured of losing all your possessions. Don't ever ask yourself why the touts are being so generous and selling their secrets so cheap. You might get suspicious and wonder why they they need your few lousy dollars when they could break every bookie themselves and own Las Vegas. Believe that there is a Santa Claus after all.

Section Two

Football Handicapping Techniques

*There's a Hoosier I know from South Bend
who swears by each streak and each trend.
But it's most often his fate that he jumps on too late
thus it's his trend to lose in the end.*

10

Subjective Handicapping

Your Unconscious Computer

What is subjective handicapping and what makes it valid? By subjective handicapping, I mean the evaluating of factors within the brain (knowledge) and sense organs (feelings) as opposed to external factors, such as statistics, trends and organized objective information (systems). It is, in my estimation, the most effective approach to handicapping.

No matter which sport one considers, the same general factors are usually analyzed when evaluating an upcoming game. Any subjective handicapper who wishes to be successful must have an abundance of accumulated knowledge, including a thorough understanding of the game, the rules, player position requirements, coaching, player drafting, officiating, execution, plays, offensive and defensive formations, athletic qualities of players, training methods and the general morale of the team.

The subjective handicapper must almost pre-play the game in his mind, using his understanding of and information on the teams involved. He must be able to take all the most pertinent factors and correctly weigh and evaluate them. Most of all, he must complete this process without emotion, outside distraction, or the consideration of irrelevant factors. He must learn to recognize the decisions made by his collective unconscious mind (commonly referred to as "gut feelings," "psychic insight" or "kharma"), as opposed to mere guessing.

There are many factors that could be significant in handicapping a football game. The balance of this chapter will be devoted to an explanation of these factors. They can rarely be looked at in isolation. They are all interlocked and interdependent, which can lead easily to confusion and improper weighing, especially by the novice. Every relevant factor is consciously and unconsciously considered in respect to every other factor. It is this one quality that makes subjective handicapping most unique and effective.

Team Match-ups

Position Match-ups

This is an often overlooked factor. Most handicappers are prone to place all emphasis on the overall teams and power ratings, instead of knowing the relative strengths of each player, especially key players. The linesmaker knows what the average bettor will consider and so he sets his line to cater to this mediocre opinion. The in-depth handicapper will assess each player's assignment and his ability to execute his position against those on the opponent's teams who are assigned to restrict or neutralize him. This will allow the smart handicapper to discover the weaknesses in any match-up and anticipate the smart coach's game plan.

Buy yourself a video tape recorder, tape at least one game involving every NFL or other league team. Study the tapes like a coach and you'll not only know your players by name and position, but by performance as well. To obtain sufficient coverage, you will also need to subscribe to cable TV or purchase a satellite dish.

Relative Strength of Players

This factor is especially significant in college football where there is less parity; however, it still applies to the pros. It never hurts to know the physical strength, body weight and speed of each player. Consider groups of players together (i.e., running backs, receivers, linemen or the team as a whole). Everything else being equal, strength, speed and weight will dominate.

Offensive and Defensive Style Match-Up

When two teams play each other, the style of play used by each team dictates the action. Balanced offenses or defenses playing teams which feature pass- or rush-oriented offenses are standard factors considered by the majority of handicappers. But the linesmaker knows these combinations and sets the line accordingly. In other words, there is no decided edge to consider these factors in a simplistic fashion. The advanced handicapper knows that he must be aware of all the offensive and defensive formations and plays, as well as the strong and weak positions on each team. He knows the options the coaches may use under varying conditions. He is able to anticipate and predict the nature and flow of the game by recalling similar match-ups in the past.

Dominance

Sometimes a team seems to dominate in certain match-ups or situations. It's reassuring to know a certain team can rise to the occasion. Much of the the time this is due to attitude or psychological factors. Try to isolate the cause. Is it because of a rivalry, the coach, the need to win or other factors?

Location Factors

Home Team vs. Away Team Match-up

This factor is often overemphasized by the amateur handicapper. This is especially true when considering the away team. How many successive games they have been away, away from their families, home cooking and the familiar? Change of playing surface and climate, weather, quality of competition, momentum, recent performance and many other factors must be considered along with home vs. away records. The home team factor is much more significant in college competition than in the pros. Fans are usually more emotional, rivalries are more frequent and glory takes on an added dimension.

Home Field Advantage

Here we are talking about being familiar with the surface and distinct characteristics of the field. How new and firm is the artificial turf? What are its footing characteristics? What type of grass and how lush or sparse is it? What type of soil is its foundation and how will the weather affect a particular surface? What effect will these considerations have on both teams? Home field advantage is often overrated by the handicapper. The linesmaker may give it a flat three points on average, but he often is just catering to public opinion. You don't have to! The value of the home field is relative. A pick 'em game should never be assessed as many points for the home field advantage as a game where the home team might be favored by 14 points. If I were making a line, I would allow no more than one or two points to the home team in an even match up, whereas I might allow four or five points if the home team were two touchdowns stronger.

Change of Surface

Some handicappers place too much stock on this factor. It is a factor, but its importance depends on other contributing factors. Does the team being considered have the option of practicing each week on the type of surface they'll be playing on this weekend? You'd better find out before you weigh this factor. Many teams, especially in the pros, now have both artificial turf and natural grass practice fields. Most home fields with artificial turf also have a grass field for practice, but the opposite is not often true. It is also valuable to know how many times a team plays on each surface, whether it makes major adjustments when changing surfaces, and how many points it averages on each type of surface. It is important not to assume that a change of surface is automatically a negative factor. If a team is changing from a less familiar to a more familiar surface, it may become an advantage. Most amateur handicappers deduct points for a change of surface automatically. Winners look at each situation individually and weigh the factor accordingly.

Change of Climate

The most obvious handicap, when a team changes climates, occurs to a team that goes from a warm to a cold climate and must play outdoors (domed stadiums are neutral in all climates). Since it is obvious to you, it is also obvious to the linesmaker and he adjusts for it when making the line. Putting too much weight on this factor amounts to overhandicapping.

Extreme changes can have a major effect on a game, much more than the linesmaker dares give it. Because the linesmaker fears one-sided action, he will often compromise on what he feels is the true value of the climate change. This leaves the door open for the smart handicapper. Common sense, along with inside information on when and how the team arrived and the extent of their practice in the area are the ingredients for measuring this factor.

Home Dog

Any team, college or pro, knows whether or not it is favored in a game. This does not mean the athletes are involved in gambling, but rather that radio, television and newspapers frequently disseminate pointspread information.

No team wants to accept the role of the inferior squad in front of their friends, relatives and hometown supporters. With the underdog role comes an extra shot of inspiration. It is difficult for the linesmaker to properly adjust for this factor. He usually allows two to three points, not enough in most cases. Home dogs are just another area where the linesmaker leaves himself vulnerable to the "wise guys."

Travel

Most amateur handicappers feel that travel can have an undue effect upon the physiological makeup of a team. This is very true in basketball, somewhat true in the first road game for a baseball team, but the least true for a football team.

Underestimating the Opponent

There are many instances when a team will take an upcoming game lightly. They find themselves placing undue emphasis on previous meetings when the opponent was easily defeated. This is more prevalant in the NCAA than in the NFL. What happened before might have occurred under different circumstances. Underestimating one's opponent is never an advantage. The strong team may win, but it may also have to fight back to overcome a deficit created by overconfidence.

Emotions and Attitude

Team Attitude

If I had to select the most important factor in handicapping, it would have to be the attitude of each team member singularly and more importantly, on a collective basis. This must also include the coaches, owners and others involved with the emotions and psyches of the players. One need only recall the spirit which led to an Olympic gold medal for the United States hockey team in the 1980 Montreal Games or the victory of the San Francisco 49ers in Super Bowl XVI to understand the significance of this factor.

If a handicapper had the privilege of spending five minutes in the dressing rooms of the teams involved in a game and had the capability of evaluating the attitude, spirit, desire, cohesiveness and determination of the players, he would win a phenomenally high percentage of his selections against the spread. Look for this subjective information in everything you see, hear and read. Properly understood, this information will produce a lot more winners.

Negative team attitude is just as important as the positive in assessing the outcome of a game. Low team morale due to problems with certain players, coaches or front office personnel are extremely important. Give the opponent up to a touchdown when such problems exist.

Emotions

The general emotional level of any team at game time is an important ingredient in your recipe for selecting winners. Too much emotion of the wrong kind can be as detrimental as the reverse can be valuable. A team too keyed up is prone to make mistakes early in the game, that is, until the physical activity dissipates the excess adrenalin and anxiety. A "down" team can find itself 14 points behind a fired-up team before it can generate any momentum.

Team Support

How much the local community and media get behind a team, college or pro, can have a direct effect on the morale and attitude of a team. Athletes do function better when they are glorified and respected. On the other hand, if the people don't care, why should a player put out that extra effort? It's tough to get psyched up without a catalyst. College players don't get paid, and pro athletes give that extra effort because of the crowd response and the opportunity to receive praise and glory.

Letdown

No team can ride the crest of an emotional high for long. When a team has prepared itself for a big game and performs extraordinarily , look for a letdown in the next game. Many handicappers will back the opponent of such a team in the next game automatically. To assume handicapping is that simple is to deceive oneself. The letdown factor must be considered and weighed carefully with all the important factors.

Team Morale

Player, coach or front office dissension can ripple through a team like an epidemic. Football (or any other team sport) requires coordinated teamwork to realize the most positive results. When team morale is low, this necessary coordination is absent. When team morale is high, on the other hand, a team can perform like a finely-tuned watch. For these reasons, team morale should be carefully assessed before making a play.

The Standings

League, Conference and Divisional Standings

This factor takes on increasing importance as the season progresses. When a team is out of the race, they have also lost heart and the players are more careful to protect themselves from injury. The more meaningful a game is to a team, the more effort they will make, and the more weight the handicapper should place on this factor.

Need to Win

This factor is closely related to the standings factor just mentioned. However, there are other reasons besides standings that may create a need to win...It could help keep the coach's job, set a record, etc.

Weather

Field Condition

Field conditions at game time can vastly affect the outcome of a game. The San Francisco 49ers usually practice all week before home games on a field that is muddy, slippery and sloppy. This is particularly true when San Francisco is having exceptionally rainy weather. The team that practices on a field that simulates the expected field condition of an upcoming game has given itself an advantage of up to seven points if its opponent does not do likewise. This is where information supersedes conjecture.

Weather

The weather can play an important role in a football game. Inclement weather (rain, sleet, snow, cold wind) can all have a dramatic effect upon the total score, type of play and tempo of the game. Bad weather invariably dictates a lower score than might be expected under fair skies and calm weather. Bad footing favors pass receivers. A receiver knows which way he is going to move and defenders will usually lose half a step because of poor footing. Cold weather favors the pass defenders because the ball becomes rock hard and more difficult to throw and catch. Ball carriers are restricted from making fancy and deceptive moves and the defense is waiting with open arms for easy tackles. Inclement weather dictates more rushing, fewer receptions, more interceptions, fewer first downs and a middle-of-the-field type of game. However, there are exceptions to this general scenario. Bad weather can open a game up because of frequent turnovers, breaks and sheer luck.

Performance Factors

Team Performance

When evaluating team performance, more must be said than just that a team is playing well, mediocre or badly. The smart handicapper wants to know *why* a team is performing as it is. Is it because of injuries, conditioning, coaching, athletic limitations, cohesiveness or team attitude?

Performance to Date and Recent Performance

These factors should never be considered independent of each other. The importance of the overall performance of any team since the season began has its most significance when measured against the team's recent performance. Know whether or not a team is playing over its head or below its ability. Look also at a team's attitude to understand its recent performance.

Momentum

Momentum has a direct relationship to recent performance, but it is not the same. While recent performance looks at overall quality, momentum also considers luck, breaks and team attitude. Recent performance may prevail and sustain itself while momentum may collapse.

Current Trends

Certain trends must be considered by the subjective handicapper. Is the team playing progressively better or worse? Is the passing game improving or deteriorating? How about the rushing game? Is the team's power rating increasing, decreasing or standing still? These and other trends are worth knowing.

The Previous Game

The handicapper must assess each team's previous game. Was the team a favorite or underdog in its last game? Did it win or lose? Was the game at home or away? There are actually eight possible combinations of these three sub-factors and the handicapper should develop a subjective understanding of how each might affect the next game played. It is difficult without the aid of records and statistics to put a mathematical weight on this factor. However, one can develop a feel for the weight of this factor over time.

Passing and Rushing

This is one place where a handicapper can make use of passing and rushing statistics. Once he knows the general statistics, the handicapper can use them as a guide in subjectively evaluating the offensive and defensive performance of a team. It's difficult to remember every detail; reliance on a statistical reference base is invaluable.

Turnovers

This is just one more statistic that must be subjectively evaluated. It is always best to be aware of, not only the number of turnovers, but the circumstances surrounding the turnovers. How many fumbles? How many interceptions? What percentage of the fumbles were recovered? How were the fumbles made? Were the interceptions a result of solid defensive plays or errant passes?

Other Factors

Coaches' Philosophy and Style

The professional handicapper knows how to relate one coach's philosophy with that of his opponent's. He also knows every coach's style and capabilities. It is a good idea to keep records on what a coach does in various situations. If you know your players, player match ups and how a coach uses his players, you are a step ahead of the public and the linemaker. Know your coaches—they are your sideline quarterbacks.

Injuries

This factor is one of the most overrated of all key factors. Consider carefully the injured player's replacement and, just as important, the replacement's replacement. If the player in question will play despite his injury, the handicapper must know the extent and nature of the injury. Will the injury seriously inhibit the athlete's performance? Never lose sight of the fact that as many as 35 players or more play a decisive role in the outcome of any game. Divide the number of injured players by 35 and you can properly ascertain the percentage of the team's ineffectiveness. It's *not* like a basketball game where one player is 20% of the team. Where would you find a capable replacement for Julius Irving, Kareem Abdul-Jabbar or Moses Malone?

National Television

This factor usually has a greater bearing on the outcome of games at the college level. Professionals have been there before. Their "stage fright" and nervousness have been lessened through experience and familarity. Common sense will dictate to the intelligent handicapper what, if any, importance to give this factor.

Line Moves

For details on understanding the significance of line moves, read carefully the chapter entitled Line Analysis.

Special Teams

A good handicapper, no matter what his approach, must consider a team's "special teams." Just like the bullpen on a baseball team's pitching staff, special teams can have a significant part in the outcome of any game. Take the time to familiarize yourself with these players and their performance.

How to Become a Loser-Suggestion #10

Increase your bets when you are losing. Believing the illusion that if you press hard and long enough you'll get it all back will assure that you will achieve your losing goal. Pressing is usually accompanied by anxiety, fear and lack of confidence, all of which collaborate to guarantee that you will lose. As long as you faithfully apply this simple technique, you'll never have to worry whether you'll win or lose.

11

Objective Handicapping

A Numbers Game

Objective handicapping utilizes statistics, the "numbers" measuring performance, to come up with a winning selection. As with other handicapping approaches, the success of objective handicapping depends upon proper weighing of the factors considered. After all, the recorded statistics are the same for everyone, including the linesmaker. If statistics served as precise predictions for all individuals who used them, then all objective handicappers would be winners, especially if someone discovered an exact formula for the utilization of historical data and statistics.

Suppose there was a group composed of a knowledgable sports forecaster, a first-rate statistician and an advanced computer programmer. Furthermore, assume all three were knowledgeable about the game of football and the teams. I'm sure that, with a dedicated effort, they might come up with about as accurate a line as is conceivable. Since this line would be their private property, they might find betting edges by comparing their line with the official line. The above scenario has been accomplished a number of times. However, the lines can be adjusted by the bookmakers. This activity puts the bookmakers on the defensive. Their only recourse is to compete directly by using their own computer sources or changing the odds. One thing is for sure: the bookmaker is not likely to let his margin of profit deteriorate.

Power Ratings: An Objective Approach

There are many ways of establishing power ratings, but basically they are all syntheses of several statistical categories. The factors used are generally total yards rushing (offensive and defensive), total yards passing (offensive and defensive), total time of possession (offensive and defensive), and total points scored (offensive and defensive). Comparisons between all teams in the NFL or NCAA are then made based on these criteria. The team with the greatest strength offensively and defensively is usually assigned the highest rating. This might be 100 or some other number above a league or conference average. All the other teams would then be rated downward from the top number based on their strength, producing a hierarchy of teams.

The limitation of power ratings is their generalization. They do not always indicate or pinpoint what the strongest or weakest components of a team are. One might use other known statistics or subjective information to determine whether a team is stronger on offense or defense, passing or rushing, but the power rating itself does not indicate where the strength lies. Some of this information can be obtained through the power rating approach if offensive and defensive power is rated separately. A team might have a 97 power rating overall, with a 93 offensively and a 99 defensively.

The greatest value of power ratings is found in establishing a pointspread. This process of establishing a pointspread is known as making a line. It is always better when making a line to have no knowledge of the official line. Once the line has been made, it can be compared with the betting line. If a handicapper should calculate a line as -2½ for a certain favorite and the linesmaker has the same team at -4 or higher, a bet would be placed on the underdog. In making this play, the handicapper assumes his line is more accurate than the linesmaker's numbers.

Using the Objective Approach

To best illustrate the mechanical, objective approach, I'm going to take an NFL match-up and analyze it based on objective criteria. The game is taking place on the ninth weekend of the season. Table 11–1 represents the accumulated statistics of the two teams. Team B has the home field advantage and is favored by four points. This is the first meeting of the season for the two teams. Team A has posted a 5–3 win/loss mark and is 4–4 versus the spread. Team B is 6–2 and is 5–3 against the points.

Without knowledge of the names of the teams involved, the statistics in Table 11–1 present a rather cold, impersonal picture, yet there is still sufficient evidence to draw some conclusions. The line and the power ratings indicate, first of all, that Team B is slightly better than Team A. The linesmaker probably gave Team A three points for the home field advantage and one point for a small advantage in power.

When one looks at total yards gained (line two), the difference between the two teams is only 6.75 yards per game, a little over 2% of the total. Total yards gained, however, does not take into consideration at least three other relevant factors—average yards per punt return, average yards per kickoff return, and yards per point. Team B has averaged 50 yards more in punt returns or approximately 12% more in total yardage. Team B has also averaged 27 more yards per game in kickoff returns, approximately 6% of total yardage. The third factor, yards per point, also shows an

Table 11-1

	Team (A) Away Dog	Avg. Per Game Team (A)	Team (B) Home Fav.	Avg. Per Game Team (B)	Fav. + or – Diff. Total	Fav. + or – Diff. Per Game
1. Power Rating	94		96			
2. Total Yards Gained	3,096	387	3,150	394	+54	+6.75
3. Total Yards Rushing	1,242	155	1,090	136	−152	−19
4. Total Yards Passing	1,854	232	2,060	258	+206	+25.75
5. Total Def. Yds Allowed	3,210	401	2,950	369	+260	+32.5
6. Total Def. Yds Allowed Rush	1,440	180	1,130	141	+310	+38.75
7. Total Def. Yds Allowed Pass.	1,770	221	1,820	228	−50	−6.25
8. Total Points Scored	184	23	208	26	+24	+3
9. Total Def. Pts. Allowed	220	27.5	174	21.75	+46	+5.75
10. Avg. Yds Per Pt. Allowed	16.83		15.14		+1.69	+1.69
11. Avg. Yds Per Point Def.	14.59		16.95		+2.36	+2.36
12. Total Yards Punt Return	408	51	798	100	+390	+48.75
13. Total Yards Kickoff Rtn.	520	65	735	92	+215	+26.88

edge for Team B. It becomes obvious that Team B has attained better field position in ball exchanges and has moved the ball greater distances which means more points.

Lines three and four can be used to deduce what type of game to expect. The game we are analyzing will showcase two balanced attacks, with Team A slightly favoring the ground game and Team B slightly favoring the passing game.

Lines 10 and 11 detail the yards-per-point criteria. Team A had to gain 16.83 yards to score one point, while it allowed its opponent to score a point every 14.59 yards. We can expect Team A to have poor punt and kickoff return coverage. In this game, where Team B excels in special teams, we can find an advantage for Team B of three points.

We've only examined a few of the many revelations that can be unearthed with these statistics. If we had knowledge about the actual teams involved, their coaches and personnel, their opposition in the first eight games, we could find even more meaning in the statistics presented in Table 11–1. Furthermore, there are many other factors the objective handicapper must consider before he can make valid decisions on the outcome of a game.

Some of the factors that the more sophisticated handicapper might consider along with the ones already mentioned include third down conversions, average yards gained per passing or rushing attempt, percentage of pass completions, turnovers, field goal attempts and successes, records at home and away, records on turf and grass, and many other similar factors. These statistics are readily available in the many sports-oriented publications (newsletters, tabloids, newspaper box scores, workbooks) printed during the football season.

One could continue with many additional factors, resulting in more work than one individual could accomplish without computer assistance. The irony is that even with all this information and work, one subjective factor (a late injury, death in a player's family, team dissension, the weather, an official's bad call, etc.) could nullify all this effort.

Statistics can disclose exactly what has transpired in the past, but they can only hint at what might occur in the future. Statistics are valuable and have their place in the scheme of handicapping, but they can never replace the human element of judgement. No one has developed a computer to evaluate the incalculable human spirit or the flux of the biological machine called man. It is good to have statistical tools to work with, but they are useless unless you apply them effectively.

How to Become a Loser-Suggestion #11

Whatever else you do, you must be sure not to use what is generally referred to as common sense. If it's logical, avoid it. If it makes good sense, be wary, you might end up a winner. Losers rarely ever indulge in reason or logic. Remember, thinking and losing don't mix.

12

Systems

Patterns for Predictions

A handicapping system is constructed by taking a number of statistical factors and sequential occurrences that show a consistent relationship and predicting that the relationship will continue in the future. There are many people who swear by some system they've found or developed. I've yet to meet one who has successfully used such a system to make any sizeable amount of money from the bookies, although a number of these individuals have done well selling books on the subject.

I'm not saying that systems are useless or don't work. I personally have tinkered with systems in games of chance and have long been convinced that systems are limited at best. My experience with craps was mentioned in Chapter 1. When applied to football, I think they have an additional weakness. They completely ignore the human component that is a critical element of team sports.

Believers in the system approach will reject my association of systems to beat games of chance with a football game. They will contend that a football game is not like a pair of dice. Granted, the more intricate the system, the more plausible it seems, but my point is that systems are just suppositions supported by the illusion that what happened before is going to continue to happen again.

I'm not categorically stating that all systems are invalid. Even the most simple has some validity and may produce over 50% winners versus the spread. The system may continue to produce over 50% winners so long as the linesmaker ignores the factor upon which the system is based. However, when the linesmaker finds too many people using the same principles and factors to beat the line, he needs only make an adjustment to defeat the system. Publicizing any system that works is the most rapid means to its demise as a successful wagering tool.

Although there are a few systems analysts who I respect (namely Barbara Nathan, Jim Longnecker and Gary Anderson), I believe that most of their systems are less valid as future predictions than they were historically. In the majority of cases I've checked, the system ends up producing much closer to 50% than the historical ratio. Remember, the system player doesn't really know if the linesmaker adjusted for the principle they adhere to since the time the system was devised. The spread that was beaten is not always the spread that is yet to be beaten.

The sophisticated system creators do have some things in their favor. First of all, the linesmaker lags behind in his adjustments, because he must usually consider a multiplicity of factors before putting up a number. Secondly, the smart or big money still has the greatest influence on the line and it is generally not guided by any system.

If you are looking for and will be satisfied with about 55% winners (enough to beat your bookie), you might consider following one of the systems publications by the authors mentioned earlier. There is no guarantee, but strict adherence to their systems could make you a modest winner. Keep in mind that deterioration of win percentage can be expected over time. Wise system promoters usually adjust or devise new systems which are more current and productive.

If the strict adherence to a system does not appeal to you, consider them as just one more subjective factor when handicapping. If the conditions are the same as those that existed when the previous games were played and it does not appear the linesmaker has made any pointspread adjustments, the validity of the system is maintained.

Systems *can* be valid and worthwhile on a limited basis. Overall, systems are as good as mechanical handicapping and are a lot less work. If you find some apparently strong systems, support them with knowledge of the game and good subjective handicapping. The win ratios of your systems should increase. The only remaining question is this: Are the systems really valid if they are modified by other nonsystematic factors?

How to Become a Loser-Suggestion #12

Look for a consensus of opinion on your plays. Using a consensus implies that the majority must be right. This is not necessarily true. The odds are that whoever engineered the direction of the consensus was after everybody's money. The more lopsided the consensus, the greater the chance you have of becoming a loser if you join the crowd.

13

Trends

Ups and Downs

Most handicappers use trends and the analysis of trends as an adjunct to the other methods they use predominantly. Trends, as they apply to handicapping football, are implied directions of improvement or decline in specific areas of performance. Awareness of trends can be quite helpful in analyzing a team's present and future performance. However, trends can flatten out or reverse themselves at any time and can, consequently, become a trap as well as a asset to successful handicapping. The best way to avoid the traps is to take several trends and utilize them collectively. The handicapper then makes his assessments based on the overall picture.

To best illustrate how trends can be tracked and utilized, I will present two hypothetical opposing teams approaching their sixth game of the season. Team A is the visiting team. Team B is at home and has been installed as a seven-point favorite. Team A is 2–1 at home and 1–1 on the road. Team B is 4–0 at home and 0–1 on the road. Table 13–1 includes a number of important factors, though a number of additional statistics could be included.

Trends are evaluated as + or—, based on the improvement (+) or decline (-) from week to week.

Table 13-1

TEAM A - Away Dog
TEAM B - Home Favorite   * Rounded off to the nearest 10 yds

Team	Factor	Wk 1	Wk 2	Wk 3	Wk 4	Wk 5	Trend*
A	Off. Yds Rushing	102	115	136	135	167	+1+2−1+3=+5
B	Off. Yds Rushing	141	178	155	151	140	+3−2−1−2=−2
A	Off. Yds Passing	180	172	218	213	196	−1+3−1−2=−1
B	Off. Yds Passing	155	140	169	232	185	−2+3+6−4=+3
A	Total Off. Yds	282	287	354	348	363	−1+6−1+2=+6
B	Total Off. Yds	296	314	324	384	325	+2+1+6−6=+3
A	Def. Yds Rushing	163	141	178	117	132	+2−3+7−2=+4
B	Def. Yds Rushing	127	139	160	144	171	−1−2+2−3=−4
A	Def. Yds Passing	199	180	175	240	210	+2+1−8+3=−2
B	Def. Yds Passing	127	135	130	170	163	−1−1−4+1=−5
A	Total Def. Yds	362	321	353	357	342	+4−3−1+2=+2
B	Total Def. Yds	254	274	290	314	334	−2−2−2−2=−8
A	Final Score	27/24	21/14	28/31	17/21	24/17	+5/−1
B	Final Score	14/21	34/27	28/27	16/14	31/23	+2/+1
A	Win/Loss	W	W	L	L	W	+1
B	Win/Loss	L	W	W	W	W	+3

You see from the rightmost column that offensively, Team A is improving in rushing (+5) while showing a slight decline in passing (-1). On the other hand, Team B is in a slightly negative trend rushing (-2) and a modest improvement trend passing (+3). In overall offense, Team A is improving twice as much as Team B (+6 compared with +3).

Defensively, Team A is +4 in rushing, -2 in passing and +2 in total defense, while Team B is -4, -5 and -8 respectively. The trends show Team A, the underdog, to be improving modestly in defense, while Team B shows a strong negative trend in defense. Team A also shows an increase in scoring, while its defense contains the opponent. On the other hand, Team B shows a weak trend toward increasing its scoring and a tendency to allow slightly more points.

An easier way for many handicappers to utilize the scenario in Table 13-1 is to depict the trends on a graph. Figure 13-2 is an example of such a graph. This and other similar graphs can be transferred onto clear plastic with a grease pencil. By overlaying these graphs, one can visualize all the trends simultaneously and make an accurate subjective assessment of the overall picture.

If a handicapper kept such graphs on a number of different factors, all kinds of match ups an easily be viewed and evaluated. If you are a subjective handicapper, graphic trends can be a useful quick reference tool.

There are a some rather successful handicappers who use trends and their analyses as the sole or primary selection tool. Although trends are probably the most valid use of statistics and objective handicapping, they probably should not be used independent of other key factors.

Figure 13-2

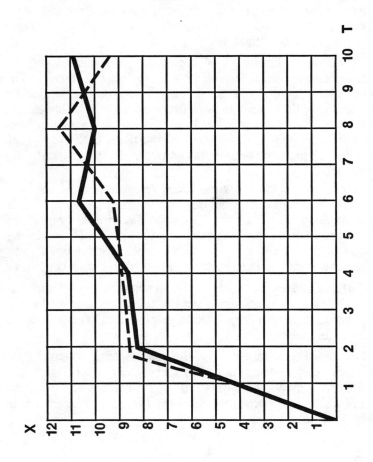

How to Become a Loser-Suggestion #13

When you receive good information, such as an injury report, a weather report or any other intelligence, be sure it is common knowledge before you bet. Then you can be assured that the linesmaker has already adjusted for it and eliminated your winning edge. Be on the lookout for rumors and insignificant gossip about sports. It puts you with the majority and we all know that the majority are losers. Don't try to be different. You might end up a winner and lead a lonely life.

14

Line Analysis

What's Coming Down?

The betting line, as a handicapping tool, is one method of prediction used by very few individuals. There are a few obvious disclosures that line moves may indicate. It is not the obvious that I wish to dwell on or emphasize. There are many subtleties that the betting line can reveal to the sharp handicapper. Unfortunately, only those who live in Las Vegas or have access to the necessary information from someone who does can realize the true benefits of "reading" the betting line.

It is a common assumption among many sports bettors that if a betting line moves it moves because more money is being bet on the side that represents the direction of the move. If a line moves from -2½ to -3, it indicates that more money is being bet on the favorite then the underdog. However, this is only a generalization and may not always be true.

Let's look at other reasons why a betting line might move.

1. There may be some late-breaking information regarding the game. This could concern injuries, internal problems, a player problem, unusual weather conditions or a number of other causes. It is up to the handicapper to discern why the line moved.

2. If only one bookmaker moves his line to balance his action, it may be of little significance. On the other hand, if the linesmaker or all the Vegas books move a line, the event should not be ignored.

3. The linesmaker is never absolutely sure he has put out the right line. Early adjustments may be necessary to assure balanced action.

4. Sometimes the linemaker is privy to relevant information before it becomes generally known. He then may put out a line commonly referred to as a "trap." Bettors in general are prone to jump on such a lopsided line and end up with the worst of it when the line moves and the word gets out. "Trap" lines are becoming rarer because pertinent information is more quickly disseminated.

Remember that the line is created to split public opinion; the betting line is not necessarily correct. What it does represent is the average opinion, in terms of money bet. The sharp handicapper, using his knowledge and information, does more work than the average bettor and concludes that the line is "wrong." If the sharp handicapper's preference should become known, the line might move.

The vast majority of all bettors are completely unaware of outlaw or early lines and thus have no way of tracking the betting action that led to the line they are offered. Any sizeable bettor who does not buy his selections from a reputable sports service should at least purchase a good line service. The price per month might be only a fraction of his usual play and, if he is a competent handicapper, I cannot imagine him not taking advantage of such information. Perhaps no other tool is of greater significance to a sports bettor.

Allow me to typify a situation where a handicapper might benefit from knowing the opening line, subsequent moves, and the closing line. Say a football line on an NFL game opened on Monday at -3 and subsequently fluctuated from -3 to -3½, back to -3 and closed at -2½. Let's also suppose that no substantive information was released during the week to account for this line behavior. Obviously, it had to be money flow. But why? Since the average player doesn't know why, or worse, never knew it took place, he is forced to ignore it and proceed to bet on the basis of his handicapping. To anyone who understood line analysis, the line movement would indicate that the early "smart" money went on the favorite, but late "smart" money went on the underdog, and in more sizeable proportions. My experience indicates, that were this situation to occur 100 times, the underdog would win at least 60 of those encounters.

In Las Vegas, the smart handicapper and player has the opportunity to study opening lines at a number of sports books and track all subsequent moves. His first step, and it is a big one, is to observe various patterns in these lines and their fluctuations. His second move should be to look for significant and consistent relationships between these line fluctuations (when, where and how much) and the results of the games concerned. Once he has a handle on it, what has he accomplished? If he has done a good job, he has discovered where the smart money is going and where the public money is being placed. He has uncovered the best handicapping available and need not look at any other objective factors. Properly employed, and coupled with good subjective handicapping, the handicapper understanding line analysis cannot help but be a substantial winner.

There is a lot more to line analysis than the limited examples and explanations I've given here; I leave it to the reader to pursue this potentially profitable area further on his own.

How to Become a Loser-Suggestion #14

Bet on your favorite team, regardless of handicapping that might suggest the contrary. You can further increase your losses by betting most when they are the biggest underdog. You will know you've given your team moral support and it will make losing more palatable.

15

Unorthodox Handicapping Methods

Stars and Tripes

I don't know how many other methods not already covered exist in the world of predicting football game winners, but I will cover a couple methods that have gained prominence among some of those looking for the secret of uncovering winners.

The first method I will discuss is the biorhythmic method, while the second and somewhat a correlative of the first, is the astrological approach. I do not lend much credence to either approach, but I will try to shed a little light on them.

Biorhythms are based on three dominant cycles of different biological duration that supposedly exist in all humans. The cycles are broadly classified into three major divisions or independent cycles. The three cycles are the physical, the emotional and the intellectual. These cycles begin at birth and are, more or less, of fixed duration. Each cycle is of different length and graphically appear as a wavy line, representing peaks and valleys. Since the three so-called cycles are of different duration (though each are approximately a month), their representative graphic lines cross and coincide at irregular positions along a continuum of wavy lines.

According to supporters of the biorhythm theory, when the cycles all match at a peak or valley, then the person they represent is either at peak capability or the opposite, respectively. However, usually the three cycles cross at different points. Seldom do they all coincide at a peak or valley. Consequently, most of the time the person being evaluated is in some intermediate state.

How are biorhythms used to handicap team sports? First, one must know the date and time of birth for each team player (when available.) Next, it is necessary to graphically illustrate the biorhythm of each player. Third, the handicapper has to compare the cycles of key players on each team. Fourth, he must collectively assess the biorhythms of one team with those of the opposing team. Finally, he must assess values of proven relativity to his findings and draw conclusions as to which team will dominate on the day of the game.

Some of the questions that this method poses to the discerning handicapper are: What scientific basis, if any, does one use to determine the exact length of a cycle? Even a few hours' error in cycle duration can drastically affect the coincidences of when the cycles reach their highs and lows. How are standards set? With so many players on a team, how can anyone assign a cumulative positive or negative value to each team and judge how these values relate to other factors?

It is my personal contention that if one were to follow biorhythms in lieu of all other factors, one must end up 50/50 in the long run. I've tried to obtain details from supposed biorhythm players, but I have not received any conclusive evidence supporting the validity of the biorhythm approach. I do believe there are biological cycles that affect us, but that the scientific evidence making them sufficiently accurate for prediction is still lacking.

Another unorthodox approach to handicapping is the astrological, horoscope method. If you wish to place your money on the stars, you cannot end up worse than 50/50 and if you can afford the juice, at least you can enjoy some good entertainment. Any form of guessing will give you a 50% winning record in the long run. Only a talented, knowledgeable handicapper consistently does better than 50%.

If you believe in the occult or the stars, enjoy yourself. The worst that can happen is you might get a little unlucky. If I were a bookie, I would love to take your action and then we'd both be happy.

How to Become a Loser-Suggestion #15

The best homework the loser can engage in is no homework at all. Don't listen to or read any information that might be important in determining the outcome of a sporting event. Put yourself in the same frame of mind you'd be in if you knew you were watching a delayed telecast of a game. The game is over but you don't know the outcome so you can enjoy the action. Try to find someone to take your action on the losing side. Not doing any homework before you play will give you a similar opportunity to lose.

16

Totals Handicapping

Overs and Unders

There are many similarities between handicapping totals and handicapping the pointspread. The key factors used in both instances are in many cases identical. There are also many other key factors used more or less exclusively for handicapping totals. These factors will be considered roughly in order of their importance.

Establishing a Line and Score

Just as in pointspread handicapping, the totals handicapper must create a line for a game he is considering. In the process of coming up with a point differential, the handicapper should also consider the number of points each team might score. A handicapper who understands the various styles of play and coaching philosophy of a team should be able to anticipate the game plan and deduce a scoring scenario. However, there are many other factors which must be taken into consideration before a total score can be predicted accurately.

Average League Score

Beginning with the second week of the regular season, the totals handicapper can establish a base number by finding the average score per team in the league. In order to obtain this average, the first week's game scores are totaled and divided by the number of games. Each subsequent week, the total scores for all games to date are averaged and a new league average is established. This average is a mean number from which the handicapper or linesmaker can proceed. This average number has increased in recent years, due to rule modifications and changes in playing styles.

Average Conference, Division and Team Scores

If there are significant variances between these averages and the league average, they could be important to predicting the total of an upcoming match up. Variances of more than a point should be explained in terms of style of play, coaching philosophy or other factors.

Yards Per Point (YPP)

The average number of offensive yards it takes a team to score one point or the number of yards a team's defense forces its opponent to acquire before allowing a point is as important to totals handicapping as pointspread handicapping. These figures should be computed weekly. The YPP factor can give insight into team attitudes, coaching styles, team maturity and execution.

Climate Change

Climate changes can have a definite effect upon the game plan and the physical effectiveness of many players. A sea-level based team might find the altitude in Denver quite tiring late in a game and will either have to plan for or adjust to it. A warm climate team playing in the northern climate late in the season could be unduly distracted by the cold, resulting in a sub-par performance. An astute handicapper keeps records on this factor and refers to them when the situation dictates.

Playing Styles

It behooves the handicapper to learn as much as possible through reading, research and game viewing. The latter can be accomplished either by acquiring a video tape recorder or obtaining access to cable and satellite television. Review games several times, playing and replaying sequences within a game several times. Observe the offensive and defensive formations, noting when and how they are used. Key in on how individuals play their position. It is up to you to learn as much as you can about these factors.

The usefulness of this type of knowledge can be seen through reference to a hypothetical example. If Team A has a strong pass offense and its opponent, Team B, has a weak pass defense, you can expect Team A to score high. If Team B, on the other hand, plays a strong ground game and scores 17–21 points a game, the total score of this game could end up anywhere in the 37–53 range.

With 28 teams in the NFL and over 100 major colleges, there are dozens of style combinations to learn. Nothing takes the place of knowledge and hard work in this area.

High and Low Numbers

The average number of points scored in an NFL game was approximately 41 in a recent year. The following conclusions were presented to me by my computer programmer John Selle.

1. Over the three years studied (1980–82), in the games where the opening line was over 41, the actual total score ended up 42 or higher 85% of the time. This *does not* mean that 85% of the games with opening lines over 41 ended up over the actual totals number. A 47 might have been the opening line and game could have ended up 45, but 45 is higher than 41, so it was included in the 85% classification.

2. The converse of the first point was also true. Approximately 85% of opening line numbers below 41 ended up 40 or lower.

3. The higher the opening line was above 41, the more prone it was to go over. The lower the number below 41, the more likely it was to go under. Playing the highest total on the NFL card over and the lowest number under produced around 70% winners in the three years studied. The linesmaker is afraid to put the "right" number on a game because the average bettor will tend to play under a very high number and over an unusually low one. The linesmaker's job is to find a number that will split the betting action. Although two strong offensive passing teams (both weak against the pass) could score 70-80 points, the linesmaker, as of this writing, has never posted a number of 60 or higher on an NFL game. The reverse is also true. Two rushing-oriented teams with strong defenses could score 20 or less points, but the linesmaker cannot post such a low number without encouraging lopsided action.

4. The frequency of occurrence of certain totals numbers is another factor to consider. According to a computer study of 607 games, more games ended up with a total score of 37 than any other number. The most frequent numbers were:

Total Score	# Times	%
37	34	5.6
31	29	4.7
34	27	4.4
45	23	3.7
47	23	3.7
51	22	3.6

Within the above range of numbers, some of the less frequent numbers were 32 (4 times), 39 (5), 35 and 36 (9 each), 42 (8) and 46 (5). The scoring system in football favors certain totals. If a handicapper decides that a game will exceed a 37-point line, he had better figure the game will go over 41 because 38, 39 and 40 are not likely to occur. Similarly, if you want to go over a line of 36, you would have an excellent chance of hitting 37, the most popular number.

Weather

The weather plays a much more important role in totals than it does in the pointspread proposition. Except when there is a large disparity between two teams, perhaps seven points or more, inclement weather has little effect on the pointspread. Real bad weather (rain, sleet, snow, cold or wind) will tend to keep the game between the 20 or 30 yard lines and the scoring low. Obviously, inclement weather favors an under play. If you can get down early, you are more likely to get a good number.

Handicap the severity of the weather against the style of play expected and the betting line you have established. Say you create a totals line of 45 on a game and the linesmaker comes out with a 41. Late weather changes indicate the game will be hampered from a scoring standpoint. Originally you had four points going for you, but now you've reevaluated your opinion and have decided the game will not be as high-scoring as originally predicted. However, this does not mean the game is an automatic under play. If your criteria for a play is a four point deviation from the linesmaker's number, you would have to re-handicap the game down to 37 before you could make an under play.

Keep in mind that bad field conditions usually favor the offense. Receivers can get a half-step on defenders when they change directions, while running backs can cause tacklers to slip. Fullbacks are not quite as effective since they usually plunge into the arms of linemen and linebackers.

The weather can force coaches to change their game plan, which can drastically affect the outcome of any game. It can be a very important factor when it applies. Don't miss any opportunity to take advantage of the weather.

Line Moves

Betting lines may move for several reasons—injuries, weather, money, etc. A handicapper must know why a line moves before he makes a play on a pointspread or total. If a line moves a half-point once or twice during the week, it merely indicates the flow of the action. It is the drastic moves (1½, 2 or more points) that require intelligence to determine the cause. If you cannot determine the cause of a line move, or are in doubt, pass the play.

Historical Factor

History doesn't necessarily repeat itself. There are always circumstances that bear consideration beyond what took place two months ago, last year or in the last ten meetings. You must look at all the factors, where they last played, weather conditions, injuries and much more. If a given match-up went over the last three meetings, find out why. Is the totals line the same? Has it been raised? Do you anticipate any changes in game strategy?

The linesmaker will usually adjust upwards on a rematch if the teams went over the last time they met. He must do this because the average bettor only looks at a handful of factors, one being that the teams will repeat. The flip-flop angle usually pays off 60% or more of the time in totals rematches. If they went over the last time, they are likely to go under the next time. The reverse is not quite as true and an under will more likely go under the next time.

Coaching Philosophy

Knowing your coaches and their philosophy can be helpful in making a decision on a totals play. A coach who knows he is being scouted for next week's game may deliberately alter his regular game plan in order to manipulate another team's strategy.

Perhaps a team is playing a lesser-quality opponent and finds itself in command of the game. Suppose the team is playing one of the strongest teams in the league the following week. A smart coach may subtly or drastically alter his formations and play sequences in order to mislead an upcoming opponent.

Need to Win

The need to win may be an important factor in totals handicapping. The knowledgable handicapper has the edge here. He must know how both coaches will play the game. Will the need to win be manifested by a shored-up defense and a cautious, ball control offense or will it fire up the team so they play a hard hitting game? Only your knowledge of the coaches and the history of the teams will help you here.

Playing Surface

Everything else being equal, more points seem to be scored on artificial turf than on grass, especially if the weather has been bad. On artificial turf, there are more turnovers, more injuries and better footing for receivers and running backs. Additionally, water drains off the field faster and sprinters run faster. All these factors tend to open up the game and lead to a higher score. Check your records to find out just how the teams in any match up have fared on different surfaces in the past.

Injuries

The linesmaker will adjust the pointspread and over/under number if he thinks the the general public will follow their usual pattern of overcompensating for injuries. Know your players, the whole roster. Keep in mind that in the NFL a backup player is usually almost as good as the first-stringer and additionally, he knows this is his one big opportunity to demonstrate his talents.

Recent Performance

How have the teams under consideration been scoring lately? Why did they score a lot of points or just a few points? It is imperative that the handicapper analyze the previous games. Did injuries, penalties, good or bad breaks, weather or other factors have an undue effect on the recent games? What is the overall strength and quality of the team? Is it improving or deteriorating relative to the league?

Betting Lag

The public seems to overemphasize overall performance, while underrating recent improvement or deterioration. If you can spot this recent trend, it can be worth up to seven points. When both teams are going in the same direction, it can be a decided edge in selecting totals play.

The totals handicapper must be aware of other subjective factors such as types of offense and defense, team attitude, relative team strengths and other factors. The emphasis when utilizing these factors should be on what impact they will have on the total score of the game.

How to Become a Loser-Suggestion #16

If you should find something in your handicapping that worked last year, ignore changes in personnel, rules, coaches, etc.

History will always repeat itself. Play it that way every time and assume that the linesmaker, bookies and everyone else with intelligence will overlook the obvious and not adjust for it.

17

Handicapping Techniques Amalgamated

Putting It All Together

The most effective handicapping approach should be one that reviews and evaluates all the techniques discussed so far in this section. Though there are as many different approaches to weighing the various techniques as there are individuals who use them, I would like to illustrate how one might proceed in handicapping an upcoming game.

Making a Line

A universal way to approach handicapping is to independently (without knowledge of the linesmaker's numbers) develop a line. You must not be swayed by outside opinions, especially the linesmaker's. With practice, experience and constant adjustments, you will become adept at finding several plays each week. Of course, it is best to test the soundness of your line on paper (or with small wagers) until you are sure it produces positive results.

The first step commonly taken when developing a line is to award three points to the home team. This may not always be accurate, but it is standard procedure with many handicappers and the linesmaker. Importance of the game to the home or visiting team may alter the three-point standard from two to four points. However, be careful when deviating.

The next step is to compare the power ratings of the teams involved. Power ratings indicate relative strengths of teams as reflected in standard offensive and defensive statistics. Some handicappers prefer to establish their own power ratings, but this is a waste of time. *The Gold Sheet* and other publications have already done this for you as accurately (or more so) than you could do yourself. Obviously at the beginning of the season such power ratings are less meaningful and almost arbitrary. As the season progresses, however, their significance increases.

The third step is to take all the relevant factors, both subjective and objective, and practice establishing plus and minus points for each factor. You will find your success directly related to your efforts and practice. Constant adjustments will be necessary until your line becomes more accurate than the linesmaker.

Once you have a line in front of you, whether it is your own or that of the linesmaker, you are ready to begin your game elimination process. Looking for plays is a twofold process. Begin by looking for reasons to eliminate games which, according to your particular method of handicapping, are obvious bad plays or "no plays." This will leave you with fewer games to study closely.

★ ★ ★

Eliminating Games

What are valid reasons for eliminating a game? Here are a few of the reasons:

1. Injuries—Injuries to key players, such as quarterbacks, running backs, linebackers and receivers can make it difficult to predict a team's performance, when that team's performance and success is hinged on that individual. The absence of a Fouts, Bradshaw or Anderson may mean the game cannot be accurately handicapped and should be passed.

2. Dissension—Unusual dissension on a team or a morale problem may make a prediction impossible.

3. Questionable Line—If the betting line is several points off from the number you expected, you must either uncover the reason why or pass the game. There are no free gifts in gambling. When you are not sure, pass.

P thats when I Bet

4. Undiscernable Edge—When your knowledge and experience do not indicate an edge on either side of a betting proposition, why force yourself to make a play? Betting such games will likely result in a 50% win-loss record.

Finding Winning Plays

After eliminating the obvious "no plays," one should zero in on plays by looking at the basic statistics relating to any match-up, including offensive yards gained (rushing and passing) and defensive yards allowed (rushing and passing). The number of yards it takes a team to score one point and the number of yards the opponent must travel to score one point are statistics which should lead a handicapper into a deeper analysis of coaching, talent, execution and other factors.

Study carefully the schedule, match up, and attitude variables mentioned in previous chapters. Use all those factors that are a part of subjective handicapping. Consider in-depth any of these that seem significant to the game being handicapped. You might consider systems and angles as factors in your game analysis, but only as one of many factors, not as a "must go" indicator.

Don't be afraid to go with your "gut feelings." Such feelings or hunches are not as arbitrary and unsupported as the term implies. If you are extremely knowledgeable about the teams and the game of football, these alleged "gut feelings" are the result of the unemotional collective mind at work.

While I have outlined the procedure for isolating plays, one step is necessary *after* the game has been played. Analyzing why you lost a game will teach you more than the celebrating of your wins. It is important to learn to be a winner by experiencing the misery and cost of your losers.

As I indicated at the beginning of this chapter, there is no one "right" way to select the winner of a football game. Whether you prefer the statistical, subjective or system approach, your success will be dependent on the combining of the various approaches to form a winning program. The proper tools (statistics, computer, etc.) can be of great help, but nothing takes the place of your intelligence and diligence in making proper use of the tools.

★ ★ ★

How to Become a Loser-Suggestion #17

Don't be conservative or try to manage your money well. This will either prolong your efforts to lose or defeat them altogether. Bet erratically, playing a lot on a particular game and less on another. You don't even have to have a reason—your hunches or your daily horoscope will serve you well enough. Whatever you do, don't keep any records. You might discover why you are losing and inadvertantly convert yourself into a winner.

Section Three

The Winning Edge

No matter what the critics will say
each man must pursue his own way.
When all's said and done, if he's good he'll have won
and the results will reflect in his play.

18

Money Management

Accounting That Counts

There exists reams of advice concerning how best to increase or preserve a sports bettor's bankroll. Much of this advice serves only to confuse the average player, discouraging him or needlessly bogging him down with mathematics and record-keeping.

In managing gambling money, a few simple rules will suffice to protect the average player's bankroll. The rules are not complicated and they are 95% as productive as the most sophisticated system available.

Remember that before any money management program can be of any value, the sports bettor must have his handicapping arsenal well-equipped and must already understand the importance of shopping for the best numbers and the most favorable odds. It is for this reason that I have postponed discussing this important subject until now.

1. Assess your bankroll. By definition, your gambling bankroll should be that amount of money you can afford to lose. It is' not imagined, desperate or borrowed money. It is not money that, if lost, would impose a hardship on yourself or your family. Look at your gambling bankroll as investment money and never overlook the possibility of a bad streak of luck and a wipe out. However, recognize that a wipe out is extremely unlikely when you manage your money as I advise.

2. Set up a plan whereby each play represents a definite percentage of your bankroll. Each play should never represent more than 5% of your bankroll; however, when starting, limit the percentage to 2%. The appropriate percentage of bankroll also depends on the number of plays to be made at one time. If you make only two or three bets simultaneously, you may safely increase the percentage to 3% or 4%. If you wish to make only one play at a time, you can safely invest an amount in the 10–15% range on that one game. Never expose to risk more than 20% of your original bankroll or 30% of your total bankroll.

3. After each day's results, recalculate the size of your next play or plays by multiplying your new bankroll by the percentage size of your plays.

Suppose you started with $10,000 and a good day netted $1000 profit. Your bankroll has now increased to $11,000 and 1% has gone from $100 to $110. Two percent would now be $220 and 5% would be $550. Do not impose a hardship on your bookmaker by changing the size of your bet by too small an increment. Increase your wager by a minimum of $50.

4. Increase your betting percentage only if:

● You are in a winning scenario. If you are betting at the 1% or 2% level, you can up your percentage play a point or two. Remember, however, that no one knows for sure what will happen in the next game. Do not get carried away when pressing.

● You have appreciated your bankroll substantially. Suppose you started with a bankroll of $10,000 and it now stands at $15,000. If your base play was 2% of the original bankroll, then increase it by adding to it 4% of your profits. In this example, we could safely wager 2% of $10,000, or $200, plus 4% of $5000, or $200. This means you could now make a $400 bet.

5. Back off when losing. This can be done three ways:

● Lower the percentage of bankroll. If you were wagering 2% on each play, reduce it to 1% when losing.

● Restrict the number of plays made at one time.

● Reevaluate your decision-making process. This does not necessarily mean you should change what was previously successful. It may only require minor changes in your handicapping procedure or a more careful analysis of your sources of information. Losing streaks, even when your handicapping is sound, are a normal occurrence and must be coped with by even the most successful gamblers.

6. Skim profits for personal use according to a plan. Determine how much profit you wish to make before allocating any of the funds to non-gambling purposes. If you started with a $10,000 bankroll, you may decide to remove money for personal use *after* you have reached $15,000. Once this plateau has been reached, you may elect to remove a percentage of the weekly profits (say 10%) for personal use. However, should a setback occur due to losses, don't remove any future profits until your bankroll has exceeded its previous high.

The important thing to remember in money management is to apply a well thought out plan. Through the application of the rules stated here, your bankroll can stay alive for an extremely long time, even under adversity. If a sports bettor can win more than 53% of his bets, than he can enjoy sports betting with his original bankroll indefinitely.

How to Become a Loser—Suggestion #18

Revert to the fantasy world so important to the normal five or six year old child. This factor is absolutely essential to the maintaining of the losing syndrome in a sports bettor. Once a player relinquishes this one losing quality, he will either cease betting entirely or start to become a winner. A loser must believe that somewhere there exists a Santa Claus, someone to fulfill his needs and desires just because he has them.

19

The Computer as a Tool

Your Statistics Warehouse

No one can deny the tremendous impact the computer has had on our society. The computer is here to stay because it reduces drudgery, increases information and opens up many avenues for discovery and efficiency.

In explaining the primary methods of handicapping, I've implied that all methods are interrelated. No one approach, whether objective or subjective, should be considered independently. However, when considering the computer, we have a unemotional and 100% objective handicapping device. Once it has been programmed (and this is the only part of the process that is subjective), it considers all information with a completely objective viewpoint. The computer output's quality and validity are no better than the human mind that conceived the programs to which the computer is slave. There's an old saying about computers that holds true in the computer handicapping field: "Garbage in, garbage out."

The usefulness of the computer to the sports handicapper lies in its capacity to store, arrange and calculate virtually unlimited quantities of information. It can almost immediately provide access to historical data covering many years and arrange it in the format most usable by the handicapper. For the systems and trends handicapper, it can test theories, look for historical patterns and determine statistical relationships, thus increasing many times the possibility of obtaining information useful in handicapping future games.

If you adhere to the statistical approach to handicapping, the computer can save you hundreds of hours of work each week and perform tasks you would not have time to accomplish without it. Should you wish to look for statistical validity to support some objective or subjective premise, the computer can analyze the information quickly, either supporting or negating the theory. One outgrowth of this type of analysis is the event system. Using the event system, the handicapper looks for sequences of events or patterns such as a given number of road games followed by a home game. These patterns are examined to uncover high-percentage win situations. This is similar to the approach used by such handicappers as Barbara Nathan and Gary Anderson.

My own use of the statistical method is limited. Trends *will* reverse themselves in time and historical patterns will not hold up forever. The computer can be an effective tool for the subjective handicapper in monitoring trends. The computer can enhance, rather than detract from, the handicapper's strength. Once the player learns how to use this tool, the computer should lead to an increase in win percentage and a savings of time.

If you are a good subjective handicapper, the computer need not compromise your technique. You will be better able to focus your attention on relevant data and will make fewer oversights and mistakes. Continued and intelligent use of the computer can shorten the decision process by arranging the material to be evaluated into easy-to-use formats.

Most handicappers establish their own or use someone else's power ratings. With a computer, it is possible to develop a number of different power ratings. One can assign relative power to different segments of the offense or defense or even to individual players. Where an overall power rating might be misleading, ratings on specific components of a team can pinpoint strengths or weaknesses.

While I have so far been concerned primarily with the positive attributes of the computer technology, it is important to recognize its weaknesses. One of the main limitations of the computer is its failure, in most cases, to consider late-breaking, pertinent information. Such information may necessitate a complete reevaluation of the game.

Remember also that unless it is programmed properly, the computer may not judge on the basis of current conditions. It does not know what the weather will be next week. It cannot foresee key injuries that radically affect your assessment. Because of these limitations, the computer can never replace human judgement.

Hundreds of programmers will develop thousands of programs (software) for the sports betting market in the coming years. Much of this material will be worthless. Beware of software that promises winners and riches. If the programs are instead sold with the understanding that they are an aid and shortcut in setting up a statistical base for handicapping, you can feel less skeptical.

Don't overuse the computer and fall into the trap of comparing apples and oranges. Don't get carried away and expect the computer to discover secrets and treasures not buried in its archives. Don't mix up your factors or misweigh them. Keep relationships intact. Be careful in comparing the statistics of two teams who haven't played each other or common teams. This holds true particularly in college football.

A well-programmed computer can illuminate those areas where public opinion is in error. But nothing good lasts forever. Soon public opinion will be sufficiently influenced by the slew of beat-the-bookie programs that the linesmaker will be forced to adjust to the new public opinion. This will put all but the very best back at square one. Your best edge is, and always will be, your departure from public opinion.

How to Become a Loser-Suggestion #19

Seek out opinions from friends, relatives, bartenders and self-proclaimed geniuses. These people are bound to bore you and lead you into making an idiotic decision. The odds are good that such an approach could hit at least a 60% losing percentage.

Section Four

Appendices

Appendix I

Glossary

Across the Board:	All games posted for wagering.
Action:	Betting. Total amount bet.
Against the Spread:	Betting against the pointspread, rather than trying to pick the winner straight-up.
Angle:	Playing a certain trend. Unusual play.
Away:	Denoting the traveling team.
Away Dog:	A pointspread underdog on the road.
Away Favorite:	A pointspread favorite on the road.
AWOL.	Busted, owes money, bankrupt.
BM:	Bookmaker.
BR:	Bankroll.
Bankroll:	Bettor's total available betting funds.
Bases:	Baseball.
Baskets:	Basketball.
Beard:	Proxy bettor.
Beef:	Argument.
Betting Line:	The odds or pointspread posted for wagering.
Big Dime:	Ten thousand dollars ($10,000).
Big Nickel:	Five thousand dollars ($5000).

Bob Martin: Former Las Vegas linesmaker, now
                                retired.
Book: Bookmaker or Sports Book.
Bookmaker (Bookie): Accepts wagers on betting
                                propositions.
The Bottom: Amount owed.
Buck: One hundred dollars ($100).
Buckets: Baskets.

Chalk: Favorite.
Chalk Player: Bettor who wagers on favorites.
Circle Game: A game on which only limited action
                                is taken.
Closing Line: Final line.
C.O.D.:   No assets.
Consensus: Majority opinion favoring one side of
                                a game.
Covering the Spread: Beating the pointspread.

Dealing: Making game available to public for
                                betting.
Dime: One thousand dollars ($1000).
Dime Line: Betting line with ten-cent spread be-
                                tween favorite (−) and underdog (+).
Dog: Underdog.
Double Dealing: Unethical sports service practice of
                                releasing both sides of its game to its
                                clients.
Due Factor: A team expected to win.

Edge: Favorable conditions.
Even Money: A bet that returns $1 profit for each $1
                                wagered.

Factor:	A condition contributing to a result, such as a football victory.
Favorite:	The team favored to win.
Fast:	Prolong a win streak.
Foots:	Football.
Future Bet:	Early-season bet on likely league or division champion.
Fuzzy:	Sure thing.
Gold Sheet:	Mort Olshan's statistical weekly.
Go With:	Bet on.
Grind:	Betting conservatively, increasing bankroll at slow but steady rate.
Half Buck:	Fifty Dollars ($50).
Handicapping:	Imposing conditions that will equalize the outcome of an event.
Heavy Action:	Extraordinarily large amount of money wagered on a particular game.
Hedge:	Making a second bet to cover another bet.
Home:	Playing in home stadium or court.
Home Dog:	A pointspread underdog at home.
Home Favorite:	A pointspread favorite at home.
Hook:	One-half point in the pointspread.
Hoops:	Basketball.
Ice Man:	Cold bettor.
Intelligence:	Weather, injury, field conditions and other information that can affect the outcome of a game.

Jock:	An athlete.
Juice:	Percentage taken by sports book or bookmaker.
Junkie:	Compulsive gambler.
Kelly Criterion:	Money management program popularized by Huey Mahl.
KO'd:	Went broke.
Lay:	Bet money on.
Lay Off:	Bookmaker betting lopsided action with other bookies.
Line:	The odds or pointspread offered for betting.
Line moves:	Changes in the betting line.
Linesmaker:	The person or persons who establish the betting line.
Lock:	A game that can't lose. (Gimmick)
Man:	Bookmaker.
Mechanical Handicapper:	Individual who uses statistics to select winners.
Middle:	Betting both sides of a propositions at different odds and winning both bets.
Minus Number:	Pointspread number indicating number of points favorite bettor must give up to win.
Money Line:	Odds expressed in dollars for favorite or underdog.
Money Management:	The systematic wagering of a bankroll.
Money Moves:	Line moves as a result of wagering.
Monitoring Service:	Independent organization devoted to documenting sports service claims.

Mush Artist:	No-pay bettor or bookie.
Nags:	Horses.
Net Units:	Amount of money units won, less money units lost including vigorish.
Net Winners:	Number of winners, less number of losers.
Nickel:	Five hundred dollars ($500).
Number:	Total score, odds or pointspread determined by the oddsmaker.
Odds:	The ratio of money that can be won in relation to money bet.
Oddsmaker:	The person or persons who determine the odds.
On the Board:	A game posted for betting.
On the Earie:	Eavesdropping.
On the Ribsteak:	Kidding, heckling, ribbing.
On the Road:	Traveling from city to city for games.
One-Sided:	Great majority of action on one side of a betting proposition.
Opening Line:	The first line posted, subject to change.
Outlaw Line:	An early "private" line established in Las Vegas by and for select gamblers.
Overlay:	A betting proposition with positive expectation.
Over/Unders:	The totals proposition, where the bettor wagers over or under a posted score.
P.P.:	Past Post, betting after the event has begun or finished.

Pari-mutuel Betting:	A system of wagering where winning bettors are paid the net pool (after taxes and breakage) in proportion to their bets.
Parity:	Equality in strength, on a comparative level.
Parlay:	Betting the proceeds of one wager on one or more additional bets.
Pick:	Select (a winner).
Pick 'em:	A football or basketball game where neither team is favored. A baseball team at even money on the money line.
Piece of Cake:	An easy win or a good bet.
Pipes:	Phones.
Player:	A person who wagers.
Plus Number:	Points a player gets when he wagers on an underdog.
Pointspread:	Points added or subtracted to a team to equalize the betting on both sides.
Ponies:	Horses.
Power:	Strength.
Power Rating:	A number representing the strength of a particular team or part of a team.
Press:	Bet more, increase one's bet.
Probability:	Mathematical possibility of an occurrence.
Prognosticate:	Predict.
Proposition:	A betting opportunity.
Punt:	Pass on a betting proposition.
Push:	A tie game, either straight-up or versus the pointspread.

Rag:	Newspaper.
Release:	A sports service selection given out to clients.
Risk:	Money exposed to loss.
Rundown:	The line on all games posted.
Service:	Sports service.
Short End:	Dog or underdog.
Shylock:	Bookie who increases the odds in his favor.
Side:	The choice of one team or another in a bet.
Snake Bit:	Unlucky, can't win.
Source:	Player's bookie.
Sports Book:	Legal sports wagering establishment.
Sports Service	A firm selling sports wagering advice.
Spread:	Pointspread.
Standing Up:	Winning.
Steam:	Too much money on one side of a proposition.
Stiff Artist:	Person who doesn't pay off.
Store:	Bookmaker.
Stroker:	Bookie or bettor who strings along another.
Subjective Handicapper:	Handicapper who prefers reason to numbers.
Sucker:	Uninformed person.
Take:	The amount won.
Teaser:	Form of parlay where bettor receives bonus points.

Ten-Cent Line:	Ten-cent differential between favorite price (minus) and underdog price (plus) on a money line.
Totals:	Proposition on the total score of both teams in a game.
Toteboard:	Public posting of teams, races and odds.
Tout:	Supposed quality prediction on the outcome of a game, or those who make them.
Toutfit:	Sports service.
Trap:	Unrealistic number or total put on a game to mislead bettors.
Trend:	A general upward, downward or flat performance movement for a team.
Trend Analysis:	Analyzing team performance by trends.
Twenty-Cent Line:	Twenty-cent difference between the favorite price (minus) and underdog price (plus) on a money line.
Underlay:	Negative expectancy selection.
Unit:	Money base for determining wager size.
Vigorish ("Vig"):	Percentage of all betting dollars retained by sports book or bookie.
Went Down:	Lost.
Wise Guy:	Well-informed bettor or handicapper.
With the Spread:	Betting the favorite.
Your Line:	Self-developed line based on handicapping.

Appendix II

Author's Recommended Reading List

Books

Anderson, Gary. *Handicapping Pro Football/The Winning Factor Approach*, Revised, 1981.

Friedman, A.J.. *Football—Picking Winners Against the Spread*, Gamblers Book Club, 1980.

Gohlke, Jim. *Sports Betting Textbook*, 1982.

Hall, Rick. *Emotional Concepts of the Sports Investor,* Ultimate Systems Investments, 1983.

Hodges, Mendelsohn and Steele. *Against the Vegas Line*, AADSS, 1983.

Jasper, Jim. *Sports Betting*, St. Martin's Press, 1979.

Mahl, Huey. *Beating the Bookie*, Gamblers Book Club Press, 1975.

Nathan, Barbara. *Money in the Bank*, Revised, 1983.

Packel, Edward. *The Mathematics of Games and Gambling*, Mathematical Association of America, New York, 1983.

Pesin, Allan. *Beating the Pro Football Pointspread*, Pinnacle Books, New York, 1983.

Reizner, Sonny and Mendelsohn, Martin. *Sports Betting with Sonny Reizner*, Gamblers Book Club Press, 1983.

Silberstang, Edwin. *Playboy's Guide to Sports Betting*, Playboy Press, New York, 1982.

Sklansky, David. *Getting the Best of It*, Gamblers Book Club Press, 1982.

Strine, Gerald and Isaacs, Neil. *Covering the Spread/How to Bet Pro Football*, Random House, New York, 1978.

Periodicals

The Experts, Ernie Kaufman, Editor; Gambling Times Incorporated (monthly).

The Gold Sheet, Mort Olshan, Editor; Nation Wide Sports Publications (weekly).

The Sports Investor, Bob McCune, Editor; Bob McCune's Sports Investments.

Sports Service News, John Hodges, Editor; American Association of Documented Sports Services.

KEEPING YOUR GAMING KNOWLEDGE CURRENT

Now that you have read *The Gambling Times Guide to Football Handicapping* and are familiar with the football handicapping methodology of Bob McCune, it's important to keep abreast of the rapid and continuous changes and developments in sports handicapping and betting, and other gambling activities. The best way to do that is with a subscription to *Gambling Times* magazine.

Since February of 1977, readers of *Gambling Times* magazine have profited immensely. They have done so by using the information they have read each month. If that sounds like a simple solution to winning more and losing less, well it is! Readers look to *Gambling Times* for that very specific reason. And it delivers.

Gambling Times is totally dedicated to showing readers how to win more money in every form of legalized gambling. How much you're going to win depends on many factors, but it's going to be considerably more than the cost of a subscription.

WINNING AND MONEY

Winning, that's what *Gambling Times* is all about. And money, that's what *Gambling.Times* is all about. Because winning and money go hand in hand.

Here's what the late Vince Lombardi, the famous football coach of the Green Bay Packers, had to say about winning:

> "It's not a sometime thing. Winning is a habit. There is no room for second place. There is only one place in my game and that is first place. I have finished second twice in my time at Green Bay and I don't ever want to finish second again. The objective is to win—fairly, squarely, decently, by the rules—but to win. To beat the other guy. Maybe that sounds hard or cruel. I don't think it is. It is and has always been an American zeal to be first in anything we do, and to win, and to win and to win."

Mr. Lombardi firmly believed that being a winner is "man's finest hour." *Gambling Times* believes it is too, while being a loser is depressing, ego-deflating, expensive and usually very lonely. "Everybody loves a winner" may be a cliche, but it's true. Winners command respect and are greatly admired. Winners are also very popular and have an abundance of friends. You may have seen a winner in a casino, with a bevy of girls surrounding him...or remember one who could get just about any girl he wanted.

Some of the greatest gamblers in the world also have strong views on what winning is all about. Here's what two of them have to say on the subject:

> "To be a winner, a man has to feel good about himself and know he has some kind of advantage going in. I never made bets on even chances. Smart is better than lucky."
>
> —"Titanic" Thompson

> "When it comes to winnin', I got me a one-track mind. You gotta want to win more than anything else. And you gotta have confidence. You can't pretend to have it. That's no good. You gotta have it. You gotta know. Guessers are losers. Gamblin's just as simple as that."
>
> —Johnny Moss

Gambling Times will bring you the knowledge you need to come home a winner and come home in the money. For it is knowledge, the kind of knowledge you'll get in its pages, that separates winners from losers. It's winning and money that *Gambling Times* offers you. *Gambling Times* will be your working manual to winning wealth.

The current distribution of this magazine is limited to selected newsstands in selected cities. Additionally, at newsstands where it is available, it's being snapped up, as soon as it's displayed, by gamblers who know a sure bet when they see one.

So if you're serious about winning, you're best off subscribing to *Gambling Times*. Then you can always count on its being there, conveniently delivered to your mailbox—and what's more, it will be there one to two weeks before it appears on the newsstands. You'll be among the first to receive the current issue as soon as it comes off the presses, and being first is the way to be a winner.

Having every monthly issue of *Gambling Times* will enable you to build an "Encyclopedia of Gambling," since the contents of this magazine are full of sound advice that will be as good in five or ten years as it is now.

As you can see, a subscription to *Gambling Times* is your best bet for a future of knowledgeable gambling. It's your ticket to *WINNING* and *MONEY.*

Take the time to read the following offer. As you can see, *Gambling Times* has gone all out to give you outstanding bonuses. You can join the knowledgeable players who have learned that *Gambling Times* helps them to win more money.

FOUR NEW WAYS TO GET 12 WINNING ISSUES OF *GAMBLING TIMES* FREE...

Every month over 250,000 readers trust *Gambling Times* to introduce powerful new winning strategies and systems. Using proven scientific methods, the world's leading experts show you how to win big money in the complex field of gambling.

Gambling Times has shown how progressive slot machines can be beat. Readers have discovered important new edges in blackjack. They've been shown how to know for sure when an opponent is bluffing at poker. *Gambling Times* has also spelled out winning betting methods for football, baseball and basketball. They've published profound new ways of beating the odds in horse racing. Their team of experts will uncover information in the months ahead that's certain to be worth thousands of dollars to you.

In fact, the features are so revolutionary that they must take special precautions to make sure *Gambling Times* readers learn these secrets long before anyone else. So how much is *Gambling Times* worth to you? Well...

NOW *GAMBLING TIMES* CAN BE BETTER THAN FREE! Here's how: This BONUS package comes AUTOMATICALLY TO YOU

WHEN YOU SUBSCRIBE...or goes to a friend if you give a gift subscription.

(1) POKER BONUS at the TROPICANA card room in Las Vegas. Play poker at the TROPICANA and receive a free dinner buffet and comps to the "Folies Bergere" show for you *and* a guest. Value exceeds $40 excluding gratuities.

(2) FREE SPORTS BET. CHURCHILL DOWNS SPORTS BOOK in Las Vegas will let you make one wager up to $300 with no "vigorish." This means instead of laying the usual 11-to-10 odds, you can actually bet even up! You can easily save $30 here.

(3) PAYOFF BIGGER THAN THE TRACK. LEROY'S RACE BOOK, in Las Vegas, will add 10% to your payoff (up to $30 extra) on a special bet. Just pick the horse and the race of your choice, anywhere in America. For the first time in history, you can win more than the track pays.

(4) OUTSTANDING ROOM DISCOUNTS available only to *Gambling Times* subscribers. Check in at the SANDS in Las Vegas or Atlantic City, the TROPICANA in Atlantic City, the HIGH SIERRA in Lake Tahoe, or the CONDADO INN & CASINO in San Juan, Puerto Rico. Stay for 3 days and 2 nights and you'll save $29 off their normal low rates.

THAT'S A SAVING GREATER THAN THE ENTIRE COST OF YOUR SUBSCRIPTION.

USE ALL FOUR CERTIFICATES (VALID FOR ONE YEAR)...GET *GAMBLING TIMES* FREE...AND YOU'LL PUT $93 IN YOUR POCKET!

To begin your delivery of *Gambling Times* magazine at once, enclose a payment of $36.00 by check or money order (U.S. currency), Master-Card or Visa. Add $5.00 per year for postage outside the United States. Send payment to:

GAMBLING TIMES MAGAZINE
1018 N. Cole Avenue
Hollywood, California 90038

GAMBLING TIMES
MONEY BACK GUARANTEE

If at any time you decide *Gambling Times* is not for you, you will receive a full refund on all unmailed copies. You are under no obligation and may keep the bonus as a gift.

Other Valuable Sources of Knowledge
Available Through *Gambling Times*
(See ordering information on page 153)

Here are some additional sources you can turn to for worthwhile gambling information:

The Experts Sports Handicapping Newsletter
Published monthly, this newsletter will show you how to become an Expert handicapper. You will learn the different styles of handicapping and be able to select the one method best suited to your personality. Yearly subscriptions are $60; $50 for *Gambling Times* subscribers.

The Experts Blackjack Newsletter
This monthly newsletter has all the top blackjack Experts working just for you. Features answers, strategies and insights that were never before possible. Yearly subscriptions are $60; $50 for *Gambling Times* subscribers.

Poker Player
Published every other week, this *Gambling Times* newspaper features the best writers and theorists on the poker scene today. You will learn all aspects of poker, from odds to psychology, as well as how to play in no-limit competition and in tournaments. Yearly subscriptions (26 issues) are $20.

Casino Marketing International

CMI sponsors the largest prize-pool blackjack tournaments in the world. Using an exciting non-elimination format, CMI offers the tournament blackjack player the opportunity to play in each round of the tournament. In 1984 the Desert Inn in Las Vegas hosted the Blackjack Tournaments. In 1985 CMI expects to offer Blackjack Tournaments in Atlantic City and Reno/Lake Tahoe. For information on where and when the next tournaments will be held, write CMI, 8462 Sunset Boulevard, Penthouse Suite, Los Angeles, CA 90069, or call toll free (800) 421-4442. In California call (800) 252-7772.

Super/System: A Course in Power Poker by Doyle Brunson

The bible for poker players. This book contains contributions from poker's leading professionals, including Bobby Baldwin, Mike Caro and David Sklansky. An encyclopedia of more than 600 pages of detailed strategy for every form of poker.

Hardbound. $50.00 (Total shipping charges: $2.50)

OTHER BOOKS AVAILABLE

If you can't find the following books at your local bookstore, they may be ordered directly from *Gambling Times,* 1018 N. Cole Ave., Hollywood, CA 90038. Information on how to order is on page 153.

Poker Books

According to Doyle by Doyle Brunson—Acknowledged by most people as the world's best all-around poker player, twice World Champion Doyle Brunson brings you his homespun wisdom from over 30 years as a professional poker player. This book will not only show you how to win at poker, it will give you valuable insights into how to better handle that poker game called LIFE.
Softbound. $6.95 (ISBN: 0-89746-003-0)

Caro on Gambling by Mike Caro—The world's leading poker writer covers all the aspects of gambling from his regular columns in *Gambling Times* magazine and *Poker Player* newspaper. Discussing odds and probabilities, bluffing and raising, psychology and character, this book will bring to light valuable concepts that can be turned into instant profits in home games as well as in the poker palaces of the West.
Softbound. $6.95 (ISBN: 0-89746-029-4)

Caro's Book of Tells by Mike Caro—The photographic body language of poker. Approximately 180 photographs with text explaining when a player is bluffing, when he's got the winning hand—and WHY. Based on accurate investigation; it is NOT guesswork. Even the greatest of gamblers has some giveaway behavior. For the first time in print, one of the world's top poker players reveals how he virtually can read minds because nearly every player has a "tell." Seal the leaks in your poker game and empty your opponent's chip tray.
Hardbound. $20.00 (ISBN: 0-914314-04-1)

The Gambling Times Official Rules of Poker by Mike Caro—Settles home poker arguments. Caro has written the revised rule book (including a section on etiquette) for the Horseshoe Club in Gardena, California, that may soon be adopted by other clubs and become the California stan-

dard. He is presently scheduling a meeting of poker room managers at the Palace Station in Las Vegas. This should lead to the creation of a uniform book of rules for Nevada cardrooms. *The Gambling Times Official Rules of Poker* includes sections of the rules from public cardrooms, but mostly it is for home poker. The book is needed because there presently exists no true authority for settling Friday night poker disputes.
Softbound. $5.95 (ISBN: 0-89746-012-X)

Poker for Women by Mike Caro—How women can take advantage of the special male-female ego wars at the poker table and win. This book also has non-poker everyday value for women. Men can be destroyed at the poker table by coy, cunning or aggressive women. That's because, on a subconscious level, men expect women to act traditionally. This book tells women when to flirt, when to be tough and when to whimper. Many of the tactics are tried and proven by Caro's own students. This book does not claim that women are better players, merely that there are strategies available to them that are not available to their male opponents.
Softbound. $5.95 (ISBN: 0-89746-009-X)

Poker Without Cards by Mike Caro—Applying world-class poker tactics to everyday life. Is the salesman bluffing? Can you get a better price? Negotiating is like playing a poker hand. Although poker tactics are common in daily encounters, few people realize when a hand is being played. It's hard to make the right decision when you're not even aware that you've been raised. The book is honest and accurate in its evaluation of behavior.
Softbound. $6.95 (ISBN: 0-89746-038-3)

Wins, Places, and Pros by Tex Sheahan—With more than 50 years of experience as a professional poker player and cardroom manager/tournament director, Tex lets his readers in on the secrets that separate the men from the boys at the poker table. Descriptions of poker events, playing experiences from all over the world, and those special personalities who are the masters of the game. . .Tex knows them all and lays it out in his marvelous easy-to-read style.
Softbound. $6.95 (ISBN: 0-89746-008-1)

Blackjack Books

The Beginner's Guide to Winning Blackjack by Stanley Roberts—The world's leading blackjack writer shows beginners to the game how to obtain an instant advantage through the simplest of techniques. Covering Basic Strategy for all major casino areas from Las Vegas to the Bahamas, Atlantic City and Reno/Tahoe, Roberts provides a simple system to immediately know when the remaining cards favor the player. The entire method can be learned in less than two hours and taken to the casinos to produce sure profits.
Softbound. $10.00 (ISBN: 0-89746-014-6)

The Gambling Times Guide to Blackjack by Stanley Roberts with Edward O. Thorp, Ken Uston, Lance Humble, Arnold Snyder, Julian Braun, D. Howard Mitchell, Jerry Patterson, and other experts in this field—The top blackjack authorities have been brought together for the first time to bring to the reader the ins and outs of the game of blackjack. All aspects of the game are discussed. Winning techniques are presented for beginners and casual players.
Softbound. $5.95 (ISBN: 0-89746-015-4)

Million Dollar Blackjack by Ken Uston—Every blackjack enthusiast or gaming traveler who fancies himself a "21" player can improve his game with this explosive bestseller. Ken Uston shows you how he and his team won over 4 million dollars at blackjack. Now, for the first time, you can find out how he did it and how his system can help you. Includes playing and betting strategies, winning secrets, protection from cheaters, Uston's Advanced Point Count System, and a glossary of inside terms used by professionals.
Hardbound. $18.95 (ISBN: 0-914314-08-4)

Casino Games

The Gambling Times Guide to Casino Games by Len Miller—The co-founder and editor of *Gambling Times* magazine vividly describes the casino games and explains their rules and betting procedures. This easy-to-follow guide covers blackjack, craps, roulette, keno, video

machines, progressive slots and more. After reading this book, you'll play like a pro!
Softbound. $5.95 (ISBN: 0-89746-017-0)

The Gambling Times Guide to Craps by N.B. Winkless, Jr.—The ultimate craps book for beginners and experts alike. It provides you with a program to tackle the house edge that can be used on a home computer. This text shows you which bets to avoid and tells you the difference between craps in Nevada and craps in other gaming resort areas. It includes a glossary of terms and a directory of dealer schools.
Softbound. $5.95 (ISBN: 0-89746-013-8)

General Interest Books

According to Gambling Times: The Rules of Gambling Games by Stanley Roberts—At last you can finally settle all the arguments regarding what the rules are in every known gambling endeavor. From pari-mutuels to bookie slips, from blackjack to gin rummy, the rules of the games and the variations that are generally accepted in both public and private situations are clearly enumerated by the world's #1 gaming authority.
Hardbound. $12.00 (ISBN: 0-914314-07-6)

The Gambling Times Guide to Gaming Around the World compiled by Arnold L. Abrams—The complete travel guide to legal gaming throughout the world. This comprehensive gaming guide lists casinos around the world; the games played in each; cardrooms and facilities; greyhound racing and horse racing tracks, as well as jai alai frontons, lotteries and sports betting facilities. This book is a must for the traveling gamer.
Softbound. $5.95 (ISBN: 0-89746-020-0)

The Gambling Times Guide to Systems That Win, Volume I and Volume II—For those who want to broaden their gambling knowledge, this two-volume set offers complete gambling systems used by the experts. Learn their strategies and how to incorporate them into your gambling style. **Volume I** covers 12 systems that win for roulette, craps, backgammon, slot machines, horse racing, baseball, basketball and football.

Softbound. $5.95 (ISBN: 0-89746-034-0)
Volume II features 12 more systems that win, covering horse racing, craps, blackjack, slot machines, jai alai and baseball.
Softbound. $5.95 (ISBN: 0-89746-034-0)

The Gambling Times Guide to Winning Systems, Volume I and Volume II—For those who take their gambling seriously, *Gambling Times* presents a two-volume set of proven winning systems. Learn how the experts beat the house edge and become consistent winners. **Volume I** contains 12 complete strategies for casino games and sports wagering, including baccarat, blackjack, keno, basketball and harness handicapping.
Softbound. $5.95 (ISBN: 0-89746-032-4)
Volume II contains 12 more winning systems covering poker bluffing, pitching analysis, greyhound handicapping and roulette.
Softbound. $5.95 (ISBN: 0-89746-033-2)

Gambling Times Presents Winning Systems and Methods, Volume I and Volume II—This two-volume collection of winning strategies by some of the nation's leading experts on gambling will help you in your quest to beat the percentages. **Volume I** includes several chapters on blackjack, as well as methods for beating baseball, basketball, hockey, steeplechase and grass racing.
Softbound. $5.95 (ISBN: 0-89746-036-7)
Volume II contains an analysis of keno and video poker, as well as systems for success in sports betting and horse racing.
Softbound. $5.95 (ISBN: 0-89746-037-5)

The Mathematics of Gambling by Edward O. Thorp—The "Albert Einstein of gambling" presents his second book on the subject. His first book, *Beat The Dealer,* set the gambling world on its heels and struck fear into the cold-blooded hearts of Las Vegas casino-owners in 1962. Now, more than twenty years later, Dr. Thorp again challenges the odds by bringing out a simple to understand version of more than thirty years of exploration into all aspects of what separates winners from losers. . .knowing the real meaning of the parameters of the games.
Softbound. $7.95 (ISBN: 0-89746-019-7)

Odds: Quick and Simple by Mike Caro—How to know the right lines and win by figuring the odds logically. Common sense replaces mathematical formulas. This book will teach probabilities plainly and powerfully. The emphasis will be on gambling, showing how to quickly determine whether or not to make a wager. Particular emphasis will be on sports bets, pot odds in poker, dice and various proposition bets. Also included will be tables of the most important gambling odds (craps, roulette, poker, blackjack, keno) for easy reference. Softbound. $5.95 (ISBN: 0-89746-030-8)

P$yching Out Vegas by Marvin Karlins, Ph.D.—The dream merchants who build and operate gaming resorts subtly work on the casino patron to direct his attention, control his actions and turn his pockets inside out. At last, their techniques are revealed to you by a noted psychologist who shows you how you can successfully control your behavior and turn a losing attitude into a lifetime winning streak. Hardbound. $12.00 (ISBN: 0-914314-03-3)

Winning by Computer by Dr. Donald Sullivan—Now, for the first time, the wonders of computer technology are harnessed for the gambler. Dr. Sullivan explains how to figure the odds and identify key factors in all forms of race and sports handicapping. Softbound. $5.95 (ISBN: 0-89746-018-9)

Sports Betting Books

The Gambling Times Guide to Basketball Handicapping by Barbara Nathan—This easy-to-read, highly informative book is the definitive guide to basketball betting. Expert sports handicapper Barbara Nathan provides handicapping knowledge, insightful coverage, and step-by-step guidance for money management. The advantages and disadvantages of relying on sports services are also covered. Softbound. $5.95 (ISBN: 0-89746-023-5)

The Gambling Times Guide to Greyhound Racing by William E. McBride—This complete discussion of greyhound racing is a must for anyone who is just beginning to appreciate this exciting and profitable sport. The book begins with a brief overview detailing the origins of greyhound racing and pari-mutuel betting, and explains the greyhound

track environment, betting procedures, and handicapping methods. Includes an appendix of various greyhound organizations, a review of greyhound books, and an interesting section on famous dogs and personalities in the world of greyhound racing.
Softbound. $5.95 (ISBN: 0-89746-007-3)

The Gambling Times Guide to Harness Racing by Igor Kusyshyn, Ph.D., Al Stanley and Sam Dragich—Three of Canada's top harness handicapping authorities present their inside approach to analyzing the harness racing scene and selecting winners. All the important factors from the type of sulky, workouts, drivers' ratings, speed, pace, etc., are skillfully presented in simple terms that can be used by novices and experienced racegoers to find the likely winners.
Softbound. $5.95 (ISBN: 0-89746-002-2)

The Gambling Times Guide to Jai Alai by William R. Keevers—The most comprehensive book on jai alai available. Author Bill Keevers takes the reader on an informative journey from the ancient beginnings of the game to its current popularity. This easy-to-understand guide will show you the fine points of the game, how to improve your betting percentage, and where to find jai alai frontons.
Softbound. $5.95 (ISBN: 0-89746-010-3)

The Gambling Times Guide to Thoroughbred Racing by R.G. Denis—Newcomers to the racetrack and veterans alike will appreciate the informative description of the thoroughbred pari-mutuel activity supplied by this experienced racing authority. Activities at the track and available information are blended skillfully in this guide to selecting winners that pay off in big-ticket returns.
Softbound. $5.95 (ISBN: 0-89746-005-7)

UPCOMING *GAMBLING TIMES* BOOKS

The following books will be at your local bookstore by September, 1984. If you can't find them there, they may also be ordered directly from *Gambling Times.*

Poker Books

Caro's Poker Encyclopedia by Mike Caro—Features alphabetical definitions and discussions of poker terms. Extensively cross-indexed, it can be used as a reference book to look up important poker terms (ante, bluff, sandbag) or it can be pleasurably read straight through. The definitions are brief; the advice is in-depth.
Softbound. $8.95 (ISBN: 0-89746-039-1)

Free Money: How to Win in the Cardrooms of California by Michael Wiesenberg—Computer expert and poker writer par excellence, Michael Wiesenberg delivers critical knowledge to those who play in the poker rooms of the western states. Wiesenberg gives you the precise meaning of the rules as well as the mathematics of poker to aid public and private poker players alike. Wiesenberg, a prolific author, is published by more gaming periodicals than any other writer.
Softbound. $6.95 (ISBN: 0-89746-027-8)

The Railbird by Rex Jones—The ultimate kibitzer, the man who watches from the rail in the poker room, has unique insights into the character and performance of all poker players. From this vantage point, Rex Jones, Ph.D., blends his expertise and considerable education in anthropology with his lifetime of poker playing and watching. The result is a delightful book with exceptional values for those who want to avoid the fatal errors of bad players and capitalize upon the qualities that make up the winning strengths of outstanding poker players.
Softbound. $6.95 (ISBN: 0-89746-028-6)

Tales Out of Tulsa by Bobby Baldwin—Oklahoma-born Bobby Baldwin, the youngest player to ever win the World Championship of Poker, is considered to be among the top five poker players in the world. Known affectionately as "The Owl," this brilliant poker genius, wise beyond

his years, brings the benefits of his experience to the pages of this book. It's sure to stop the leaks in your poker game, and you will be amazingly ahead of your opponents in the very next game you play.
Softbound. $6.95 (ISBN: 0-89746-006-5)

World Class Poker, Play by Play by Mike Caro—Once again, Caro brings the world of poker to life. This time he gives us a one-card-at-a-time analysis of world class poker, with many card illustrations. This book includes discussions of professional tactics, then simulates game situations and asks the reader to make decisions. Next, Caro provides the answer and the hand continues. This learn-while-you-pretend-to-play format is a favorite teaching method of Caro's and one which meets with a great deal of success.
Hardbound. $20.00 (ISBN: 0-914314-06-08)

General Interest Books

Caro on Computer Gambling by Mike Caro—Caro discusses computers and how they will change gambling. He provides winning systems and descriptions of actual programs. This book will give the novice a taste of how computers work. Using the Pascal programming language, Caro builds a working program step-by-step to show how a computer thinks and, also, how a human should analyze gambling propositions. This book is only slightly technical and mostly logical. Also discussed are ways that computers can cheat and speculation on the future of computers in gambling. Will you be able to type in your horse bets from your home computer? Can that personal computer be linked by phone into a perpetual poker game with the pots going straight into your bank account? The answers to these questions are found right here in Caro's book.
Softbound. $6.95 (ISBN: 0-89746-042-1)

The Gambling Times Quiz Book by Mike Caro—Learn while testing your knowledge. Caro's book includes questions and answers on the concepts and information published in previous issues of *Gambling Times*. Caro tells why an answer is correct and credit is given to the author whose *Gambling Times* article suggested the question. This book covers only established fact, not the personal opinions of authors, and Caro's inimita-

ble style makes this an easy-reading, easy-learning book.
Softbound. $5.95 (ISBN: 0-89746-031-6)

How the Superstars Gamble by Ron Delpit—Follow the stars to the racetracks, ball games, casinos and private clubs. You'll be amazed at how involved these world famous personalities are in the gambling scene, and how clever they are at the games they play. Ron Delpit, lifelong horse racing fan and confidant of innumerable showbiz greats, tells you fascinating tales about his friends, the superstars, with startling heretofore secret facts.
Hardbound. $12.00 (ISBN: 0-914314-17-3)

How to Win at Gaming Tournaments by Haven Earle Haley—Win your share of the millions of dollars and fabulous prizes being awarded to gaming contestants, and have the glory of being a World Champion. Poker, gin rummy, backgammon, craps, blackjack and baccarat are all popular tournament games. The rules, special tournament regulations, playing procedures, and how to obtain free entry are fully explained in this informative manual. The tournament promoters—who they are, where they hold events—and the cash and prizes awarded are explained in detail. Tournament play usually requires special strategy changes, which are detailed in this book.
Softbound. $8.95 (ISBN: 0-89746-016-2)

You're Comped: How to Be a Casino Guest by Len Miller—If you're a player you don't have to pay! Learn how to be "comped" in luxury casino-resort hotels the world over. A list of casinos together with names and addresses of junket representatives are included in this revealing guidebook. How to handle yourself on a junket is important if you want to receive all that you've been promised and be invited back again. How to do this, along with what you can expect from the casino, is explained in detail.
Softbound. $7.95 (ISBN: 0-89746-041-3)

Sports Betting Books

Fast Track to Harness Racing Profits by Mark Cramer—This systematic analysis of nuances in past performances will uncover patterns of improvement which will lead to flat bet profits. This book provides a functioning balance between creative handicapping and mechanical application.
Softbound. $6.95 (ISBN: 0-89746-026-X)

Fast Track to Thoroughbred Profits by Mark Cramer—A unique approach to selecting winners, with price in mind, by distinguishing between valuable and common-place information. Results: higher average payoffs and solid flat bet profits. How to spot signs of improvement and when to cash in. And much, much more.
Softbound. $6.95 (ISBN: 0-89746-025-1)

Ordering Information

Send your book order along with your check or money order to:

Gambling Times
1018 N. Cole Ave.
Hollywood, CA 90038

Softbound Books: Please add $1.00 per book if delivered in the United States, $1.50 in Canada or Mexico, and $3.50 for foreign countries.
Hardbound Books: Shipping charges for the following books are $2.50 if delivered in the United States, $3.00 in Canada or Mexico, and $5.00 for foreign countries:
According to Gambling Times: The Rules of Gambling Games
Caro's Book of Tells
How the Superstars Gamble
Million Dollar Blackjack
P$yching Out Vegas
Super/System: A Course in Power Poker
Winning Blackjack (softcover, large format)
World Class Poker, Play by Play